For Jack, Clara and family

IN SUPPORT OF
HELP *for*
HEROES

Profits from the sale of this book to go to Help for Heroes

Collated and written by Honor Rawcliffe.
Final edit version 2016.

Published by Poplar Moss Publications

ISBN 978-1-5262-0558-2

Printed by
ZPQ Designs
1-2 Back Saint Annes Road West
Lytham St. Annes
Lancashire FY8 1RD

PREFACE

I first met Jack and Clara in 1958 when we bought the house next door to theirs in Wesham. We couldn't have wished for better neighbours, they were so kind and helpful that we remained staunch friends even after we moved away several years later.

Jack never spoke about his exploits in WW2. It was only by sheer chance when we were discussing holidays, long after we had both retired, about the places he had been and how he didn't wish to return to any of them, that I discovered why. I found his tales so interesting and began asking questions. He didn't wish to write his own memoirs, so I volunteered to write them for him. I began to take notes. It was only after I gave him a copy of the first draft that his family discovered his wartime experiences.

Regretfully at that time, there was no demand for military stories, so many had been previously published and publishers didn't want to know about any more. I decided to try again to find a publisher, so in 2014 I re-edited the manuscript adding the illustrations and newspaper cuttings his mother had saved all those years ago.

Members of five generations of my own family have served in the British Forces. My grandfather and three brothers enlisted for WW1 and only two returned – both scarred for life. William died in Basra (now Iraq), and Thomas is buried on The Somme. Grandfather, a corporal, was awarded the Military Medal for bravery in France. He also fought in North Africa, Palestine, (he kept an olive leaf from a tree in the Garden of Gethsemane in his prayer book; I saw it as a child) and Gallipoli with the Royal Engineers. Their last duties were to shoot the mules and detonate the remaining ammunition before evacuation to prevent them from falling into enemy hands. I only discovered this information a few years ago from one of my cousins.

I, like so many others, have lived through some extremely austere times. I was only four years old when my father left home, (leaving my mother with four very young children) to fight in Germany with the Heavy Artillery Regiment in WW2.

One of my young brothers was a regular soldier for fifteen years with the Royal Corp of Signals, serving in the Middle East, Germany and Cyprus.

War is evil, but in defence of the Realm it becomes a necessary evil.

War is destructive. The smithy at Freckleton was demolished on the 24th September 1940 when one of sixteen bombs fell on the Fylde Rural Area. No further details of this raid were published. Kirkham residents witnessed wanton destruction on the 29th of September 1941. Eight high explosive bombs were dropped on 133 properties in Mellor Road, Orders Lane, and Moor Street, near to my great aunt and uncle's homes. This raid resulted in two fatalities, seven people were wounded and eighteen residents became homeless. Most of this information was regarded as "classified" and was not revealed until October 7th 1944 in the West Lancashire Evening Gazette. (It is now stored on microfilm at Blackpool Central Library.)

War is cruel - it doesn't discriminate. This was apparent in August, 1944, when an American Liberator bomber from Warton Air Base accidentally crash landed on Freckleton village school during a violent thunder storm. The consequences were truly, cruelly, catastrophic.

War is costly in so many ways. Not only in monetary values but also in psychological and physical terms. I only hope profits from Gunner Jack Lee will help our present day 'heroes' to achieve greater life qualities and opportunities.

CONTENTS

ILLUSTRATIONS

PROLOGUE

Brr brr. Brr brr. Brr brr.

"Hello, Grandma."

"Hello James luv, are you all right?"

"Yes thanks. Is Grandad there?"

"He's in the shed, what do you want him for?"

"Has he got a gas mask or any other memorabilia left over from the war?"

"You can take Grandad if you want, he's memorabilia. I don't think there's a gas mask but I know he's got some other bits and pieces. What do you want it for?"

"Miss at school asked us to collect things about World War Two for our history project."

"He's here now, you can ask him yourself."

"Hi Grandad, Miss wants to know if you've got a gas mask or any things left over from the war that we could put on our history project display at school?"

"Aye, I've got a few bits and some magazines but no gas mask. I'll be able to sort you something out. When do you want it?"

"Oh goody, as soon as I can have it. I'll tell Miss, she will be pleased. Ta ra, Grandad."

"Now let's see, where did I put that box with all the war stuff in?"

"It'll be either in your wardrobe upstairs or in your shed along with all your other paraphernalia. Where are you going now? Your tea's ready!"

"I'll not be long, I'm only having a look in my shed. You can be putting tea out."

"Oh well, I'll start without you if you're not back."

Hmm, she thought to herself. He said he wouldn't be long but this

hotpot's going to be cold if he doesn't come soon. I'm having mine while it's still hot.
"Oh, you're back then Jack, have you found what you were looking for?"
"Aye, it's all in here."
"Well get your tea first before it goes cold. That lot'll keep 'til later."

"That was good Clara. I'll have my cuppa tea in the other room while I'm sorting something out for James."
"Well I want to watch Coronation Street when I've washed up so I'll leave you to it."
He began to sift through the contents of the battered old box. They were all there, the memories came flooding back as he studied the faces of the brave young men in the photographs.
Then he came across the dog-eared notebook he'd brought back from Italy. Gunner J. Lee. 1086426.

CHAPTER ONE
CALL UP

Our Bob was the first to go, when he was twenty. He was conscripted during the threat of war and automatically went in 1939 to Royal Artillery training at Belle Vue Headquarters, Manchester.

Shortly after, our Bill's papers arrived; he was posted to Kimmal Park, Wales, for training in the Black Watch Regiment.

Oldest brother Harry tried to enlist, but was refused on the grounds that he had an essential civilian occupation. He worked for the London Midland Scottish Railway Company in the Goods Department in the sidings at Wesham. Kirkham and Wesham railway station was an important industrial junction and distribution point for Blackpool, the Fleetwood fishing industry and the Fylde Coast. There were also military bases nearby at Kirkham, Weeton and Warton.

It was almost the end of August 1940 before my call up papers arrived. I had been expecting them because most of the village lads my age - I was 20 in June - had received theirs.

They were there on Monday when I called home for dinner. I returned to work in the afternoon, handed in my notice and finished the same day.

When I first left school at fourteen, I was a butcher's apprentice in St. Annes. I bought a brand new bike on tick for two shillings a week, so that I could cycle the seven mile journey and save on travelling expenses. The cost of a worker's return ticket to travel before 8.00am was nine pence a day.

After six months, the firm changed hands. My original employer had been a gentleman, but my face didn't seem to fit with the new management. I was expected to deliver hand bills throughout the town after a hard day's work, so I decided to quit.

I was employed as a delivery boy at the Co-op in Kirkham, only because my mother was a member, until I was sixteen. I was promised I would then become a counter assistant, because the only female employee was leaving.

The position didn't materialise. Co-op policy changed and more women were recruited. I was very annoyed because I had missed an opportunity to be apprenticed to a local builder as a joiner.

I was unemployed for a few weeks and tried a variety of occupations until I filled a vacancy at a slipper factory. I didn't care for the job but there was little else available.

When an opportunity to work for the Co-op in the local coal bagging department arose, I took it thinking I would soon be able to transfer to counter service.

Two and a half years later, I was still with coal and John Yates was my manager. He wasn't so suited to receive my notice and tried to reason with me to stay on, at least until they found a replacement.

As far as I was concerned that was it. I'd made my mind up. I was glad to be getting out. If I was to be off to war with only a fortnight's notice, I was going to make sure I had a holiday before I went.

My medical at Preston was a bit tricky. I considered myself lucky to pass A1. I had a dropped pupil in my right eye (coloboma) which caused double vision. I had grown used to it, it hadn't caused me much trouble and I couldn't foresee any difficulties ahead. I came in for some stick from an over-zealous sergeant during training, when my eye was almost closed. He must have thought I was winking at him, but it was a natural reaction to shield it from bright light.

Later on in the desert, I had to wear protective goggles to subdue the fierce sunlight and the crystalline reflection from the sea of sand.

Most of the time prior to joining up I spent lounging about and resting. That is when I wasn't trying to find out where Marske by the Sea was. No one in Wesham had ever heard of it. I discovered it was near Redcar in Cleveland.

I was to report to the Royal Artillery training unit in gunnery and field artillery on September 12th, 1940.

CHAPTER TWO
TRAINING

My rail travel warrant duly arrived and I eventually made it to Marske by the Sea, where army wagons collected all the new recruits.

After a hot meal at the barracks we were all issued with the necessary papers, including the booklet AB64 which listed all our personal details, such as name, height and occupation. We then received our army blankets and were directed to huts where we were accommodated for the next three months.

The following day we were kitted out and the vigorous training began. It consisted of a great deal of square bashing, rhythm marching, counting, shouting and fight manoeuvres with 100lb Howitzers drawn by heavy, purpose-built wagons called matadors.

The lads in our platoon were from all parts of the country and covered a wide range of occupations.

McVeigh was the most outstanding character. He was a stocky, ginger-haired 'comedian' from Liverpool, whose main objective was to leave the army as soon as possible. Even though he had passed his medical as A1; he nearly drove our drill sergeant to distraction by trying to prove lack of co-ordination.

McVeigh was constantly out of step and whenever the command 'stand at ease' was given, he always put his left foot forwards instead of sideways. One day in desperation, the sergeant grabbed hold of his leg and attempted to place it in the correct position, but without success. We never knew what he would do next; he created many amusing diversions for us, but woe betide anyone caught laughing or even smirking at his antics.

Some of the lads once found McVeigh in an open space between the barrack square and our huts. He was going through the motions of throwing something onto the ground. When challenged, he said he was feeding the ducks, but his attempts at senility proved futile too. He was totally fearless of authority or the consequences of his actions.

Another bloke tried for discharge on medical grounds by feigning blindness. One evening however, whilst at the cinema, his medical officer occupied the adjoining seat. Recognising him, he said, “Hello, Jones, are you enjoying the film?” to which Jones replied,

“Am I on the right train for Newcastle?”

Needless to say he was dispatched forthwith back to his platoon.

'Square bashing', rifle and Howitzer training were priorities. Most of the marching and rifle practice took place on Redcar race track. We were actually billeted there, three men to a stable.

I found rifle practice rather daunting because I had to use my left eye, when really my right should have been the dominant one. It was a good job the bullseyes were positioned in front of high sandy mounds, because I was always way off target. I was thankful no-one appeared to notice and that I didn't hit anything I shouldn't have.

It paid off to be very smart on parade, especially when it was time for the duty officer to choose the four night guards. His hawk eyes missed nothing as he inspected the front and rear of the lines of men. The one he thought the smartest, he tapped on the shoulder with his leather-bound baton. That soldier was to be the 'runner', fetching and carrying messages and meals, looking after any men on jankers and following any other orders from the guard sergeant.

I was the runner on numerous occasions. I didn't mind the activities, the time appeared to pass quickly; it was often interesting and certainly a cushier number than simply standing guard. Above all, for my labours, I had a full night's sleep. The three men selected for guard duty had four hours off and two on throughout the twenty-four hour stint.

I didn't mind the 'bull' attached to army drill. Polishing all the brass buttons and buckles, cleaning gaiters, and boning the toes of my army boots with polish, a bit of spit and an old toothbrush until I could almost see my reflection in the shine.

On numerous occasions our sergeant or officers checked our boots for the correct number of studs. I thought it unnecessary but to be a stud short caused a reprimand.

As part of the normal training routine, all rifles had to be kept immaculately clean, and were constantly subjected to vigorous inspections.

Whilst stationed at Marske by the Sea, there were twenty-four men to a hut, twelve on each side. Our rifles were housed inside the door, in numbered sequence on a wooden stand in pyramid formation.

Since all rifles were numbered, each soldier was able to collect his own speedily with ease from the pyramid. Spot checks were often carried out to see if individuals had memorised their rifle numbers.

Late one evening a soldier from our platoon arrived back in the hut rather worse for drink. During the night, he mistook the rifle rack for the toilet. The following morning the air was blue because of the extra work involved, cleaning and preparing the wet rifles for inspection.

I stood many guard duties at Redcar, during which time we were often under attack from German bombers. I used to hold my breath when they came over, not only because of the danger of a direct hit, but because the racecourse was next to the gas works. I feared the enemy planes were aiming for the huge gasometer. Fortunately for us, they were off target but the racecourse copped it.

Guard duty training usually followed set patterns. Our officers crept stealthily alongside a high wall in the dark to test us. If there was no response to:

"Halt! Who goes there?" they were challenged again. When the response came,

"Friend." It was followed by,

"Advance and be recognised," which the officers were obliged to do.

During training, some of the officers were very trying and didn't speak until virtually the last second; immediately before the guards, acting under orders, were poised with fingers on triggers ready to shoot.

When off duty, we utilised the entertainment facilities in Redcar. There was a cinema and a good village hall where dances were held. It was there I experienced my first moral dilemma. Someone had stolen my gas mask. I had left it in the cloakroom hanging under my army overcoat. At the end of the evening I said to one of my mates,

"Somebody's nicked my gas mask."

Without hesitation, he replied,

"Well just take another one back." Which I did, rather than have my army pay docked to provide another, and possibly be confined to barracks too. Unfortunately the outer case on the one I took was Blanco'd green. When I returned to barracks I had to spend a considerable amount of time scrubbing the colour off.

Our gas mask covers were new, natural canvas. If it had been a soldier from the Green Howards who had taken mine, he would have had to Blanco it, but that wasn't my problem.

When general training at Marske by the Sea was completed, we performed the standard passing out parade with regimental brass band, before invited civilians as guests. Our Colonel in Chief took the salute. It was a proud day for us all.

The numbered rhythm drill had been mastered and executed with precision. There were no complaints and we were rewarded with a few days leave to visit home.

The next posting was to Watford, for further training. It was there that several artillery units merged.

We were housed in a disused church. I slept in one of the bunks upstairs in the choir area. So did McVeigh and one night, he returned lively after a few pints. He forgot where he was and fell from the choir balcony when he got out from the wrong side of his bunk. He broke a leg, and was hospitalised for a while, eventually embarking with us on crutches.

I was allowed fourteen days embarkation leave before returning to Watford, where I was issued with tropical kit. It was common gossip amongst the lads we were about to leave for India.

The train took us direct from Watford into Liverpool docks. There were no opportunities to escape for the weak-hearted, though some said they contemplated it.

CHAPTER THREE
EMBARKATION

We boarded the Viceroy of India at the end of March for a sea voyage which was to last six weeks. A few cargo boats sailed with us from Liverpool, others joined from various ports en route to Southampton. The final convoy was an impressive sight. As we left the English Channel, in all there were twenty-four vessels, including cruisers, destroyers, and battleships. We British were confident and about to show Gerry what stern stuff we were made of.

At nightfall strict black-out was enforced and all ships sailed close together from dusk until dawn. We were escorted by two battleships and flanked by eleven warships on port and starboard sides. These remained with us for protection against enemy submarines, warships or aircraft. Fortunately, these services were not required. The only incident investigated by one of our battleships was when a dot on the horizon in the Atlantic Ocean was reported. It was confirmed a neutral vessel.

The catering staff on the Viceroy of India provided excellent meals for the troops with the exception of the dried potatoes. I found them most unpalatable and certainly nothing like the potatoes back home. The freshly baked daily bread compensated, it was scrumptious, I had never tasted better.

There was a hospital and mortuary on board. Regretfully, the mortuary was required when only a few days out from Southampton. It was my first experience of death. A young soldier from the Signals Corp had actually embarked with head injuries which proved fatal.

The entire parade including the service was very moving, and the hymns chosen were sung by the finest body of men I had ever encountered. Although the sea was calm and the air still, the atmosphere was electric. Only the drone of the engine could be heard during the minute of silence, before interment to the depths. It was a sombre day, never to be forgotten.

Even though we had been issued with tropical kit, we had no idea of our destination until we were well out into the Atlantic. We were aware of trouble in Japan, that was one option, but most of the lads still thought we were heading for India. Not so - the Middle East was to be our objective, via the Cape and the Suez Canal.

As soon as temperatures began to soar, we were issued with daily bottles of quinine. I found it tasted most disagreeable, but orders were orders. It was used as a tonic, a fever cure, and to combat malaria.

Intense training activities continued relentlessly on deck, throughout the voyage. For gunnery practice we used wooden models. There were parade duties, gas mask techniques, physical education and emergency lifeboat drills. Wherever we went, our canvas lifejackets went too. They served as pillows at night as we slept in hammocks.

During the first parade duty at sea, our platoon sergeant asked for volunteers to perform batman duties. My hand shot up immediately. I thought it would be a means of escaping some of the repetitive training routines. What a let-down. There was no respite, I was to continue as normal with the training and drill duties as well as the batman tasks. I was obliged to rise earlier in the mornings to polish my officers' boots and Sam Browns (leather belts). I soon got used to the regime, it was no hardship. I had a good officer and he treated me well on pay days.

Our first port of call was Durban where we anchored for five days. The troops were billeted with local families. Two mates and myself stayed in a luxury bungalow with a Mrs Everett whose husband was serving with the South African Forces. We were well cared for and when we left, she wrote a letter home to my family dated 23rd April 1941, to say I was safe and well, en route to the Middle East. She asked Mum to forward her address to me so that I may write and visit her again if we should return to Durban.

Mrs Everett's letter home was the first indication of my whereabouts since leaving Watford. Although my parents knew I was to be posted abroad, they had no idea where. I was convinced the blanket of silence was for security reasons.

From Durban we continued to Port Tufick where we transferred to a smaller cargo boat to sail along the Suez Canal to Ismailia. The remainder of the journey by rail took us to our destination, Haifa.

Mrs Everett's Letter

260 Essenwood Rd,
Durban
Natal
S. Africa.
Wednesday 23rd April.

Dear Mrs Lee,

This is just a note to let you know that I met your son yesterday & he is looking very well. He sends his love to you & the family & says he has written.

He came to dinner with a couple of pals last night.

He left again today & I didn't think to give him my address incase he calls this way again, so would you please let him

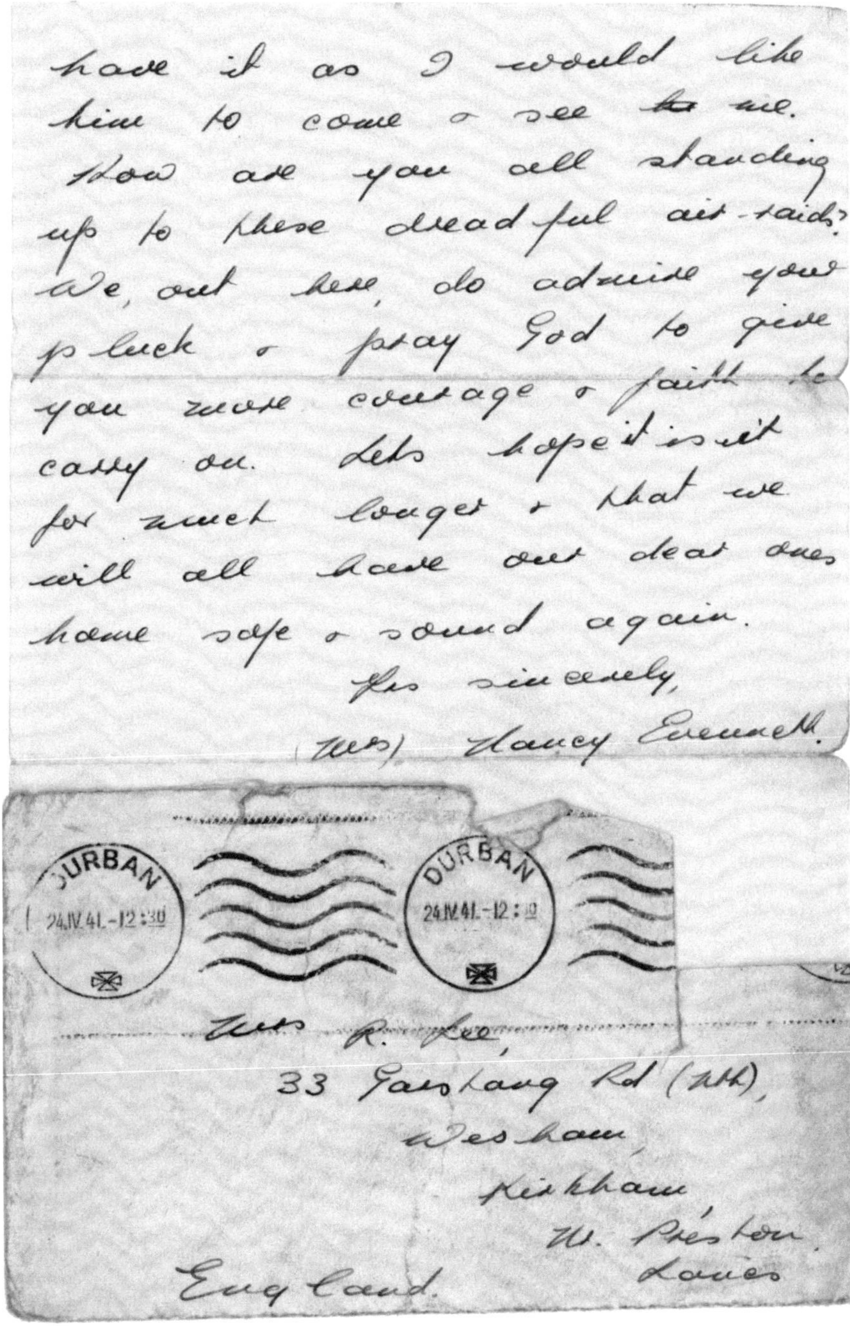

have it as I would like
him to come & see ~~to~~ me.
How are you all standing
up to these dreadful air-raids?
We, out here, do admire your
pluck & pray God to give
you more courage & faith to
carry on. Lets hope it is'nt
for much longer & that we
will all have our dear ones
home safe & sound again.

Yrs sincerely,

(Mrs) Nancy Everett.

DURBAN 24.IV.41.-12:30

DURBAN 24.IV.41.-12:30

Mrs R. Lee,
33 Garstang Rd (Nth),
Wesham,
Kirkham,
W. Preston.
Lancs
England.

CHAPTER FOUR
FOREIGN SOIL

Our regiment camped in canvas tents on the outskirts of Haifa on the Plains of Mount Carmel. The retinue attached included 'Pack Artillery' - thirty mules to transport our equipment and guns. The guns were ours, previously captured in Eritrea. We used them for training but they were eventually abandoned. My batman duties on land continued automatically at Haifa. Some of these included 'waiting on' in the officers' mess and serving drinks for which the officers signed. It was conveniently co-incidental that the officers' mess happened to be situated across the track, adjacent to our platoon tent. Whenever the opportunity arose, I was able to slip bottles of beer under the canvas to my mates. When some of the officers had had enough to drink, they hardly knew what they were signing for, and the bountiful beverage was a bonus greatly appreciated for the few weeks we were there.

Route march training was exhausting in the scorching heat on the parched plains. Topees were essential. They were very lightweight helmets made from pith or cork, covered with fine linen fabric the colour of sand for camouflage. To be caught without a topee during the day was an open invitation to warrant a charge.

On a route march one day when the heat was exceptionally oppressive, spontaneous combustion took place in a box of matches in my trouser pocket. The material ignited, burning my thigh. I doused the flames by hand, but later had the cost of a new pair of khaki drills deducted from my pay. Needless to say, I left matches behind during all further training.

The mules were most useful during training exercises, carrying provisions and equipment up mountainous tracks inaccessible to vehicles. At this time, we were informed we were on stand-by to deter skirmishes in Abyssinia. We also had ten mounted officers who rode chestnut chargers. The horses and mules were the responsibility of the Cypriot army personnel, but the regiment had its own farriers, who were constantly occupied keeping mounts shod because of the heavy workload on the undulating stony ground.

There were comical sights when the Cypriots hung onto the mules' tails to be towed, to ease their climb up the rocky paths. It was a wonder to me that the mules kept moving at all.

Some of the training took place on concrete-like ground, so parched and cracked, which only a few weeks previously had supported wheat crops. It looked so burnt and barren it was difficult to imagine.

Sometimes during evening exercises, we sheltered in orange groves, where we slept on ground sheets under blankets. It was much cooler at night. The trees were heavily laden with ripening fruit and their heady orange aroma filled the air.

The last duty before settling down was to cover any exposed area of skin with mosquito deterrent cream since they were such a nuisance and bred profusely in the tropical heat.

Other dangerous pests were the scorpions, which appeared to congregate in colonies under stones. We regarded them as the hidden enemy. They had a nasty way of retaliating whenever they were disturbed. Any stings required immediate attention.

Scorpion sport was a different matter. During leisure hours I used to watch the antics of some of the lads. They would find a scorpion and hold it down with a stick so enabling string to be attached to its tail. It was then held by the string and lowered over a pile of small rocks. When suspended this way, it was incredible to see the size of rock it was able to clasp and lift.

At Haifa, fuel, i.e., timber necessary to cook our food, was in short supply. During our training exercises we had seen logs in abundance stacked on the slopes of Mount Carmel. A few of us decided to acquire some of them and took them to the cookhouse. What we didn't know was that the logs belonged to neutral Arabs living in the vicinity. We very nearly caused an international incident.

We had been observed removing the 'fuel'. The Arab leader with six of his henchmen on huge white stallions charged into our camp, furiously demanding to see our commandant. We were ordered to transport all the logs back to where we found them. If we didn't, the Arabs had threatened to set fire to our camp. Our catering staff had to economise whilst awaiting delivery of army issue fuel, which did eventually arrive.

Our laundry at Haifa was taken care of by local civilians known as dhobies. Even though we had our own wash house for hand washing clothes, it was so cheap and convenient to have it done for us. It was an experience to watch the drying and ironing procedures. After washing the clothes by hand, the dhobies laid them out on the ground and covered them with fine hot sand to dry. Old flat irons were heated by charcoal burners. Before the ironing process on wooden tables began, the dhobi took a mouthful of water and sprayed it carefully onto the garment, which was returned neatly folded like new. We certainly couldn't have made such a good job and the cost didn't justify the effort.

The regiment had reasonable NAAFI facilities at Haifa, where we bought essentials such as soap, razor blades, sweets, cigarettes and cheap drinks. I celebrated my twenty first birthday there with a round of drinks. There were no presents and my card from home didn't arrive until well after the event. It took six weeks for a letter from England to arrive and vice versa, but it was nice to know they were thinking about me. I decided I would make up for the celebration on my next leave home.

There were a few enterprising civilian opportunists working in the NAAFI. Some of them made drinking glasses from discarded beer bottles. I enjoyed watching the process on many occasions. They simply filled the empty bottles to just below the curve of the necks with oil, into which they carefully placed the tip of a red hot poker. The glass could be heard cracking as it sheared off at the top oil level. The rough edge was then polished on a stone. I tried it myself and was amazed to find it really worked.

During off duty hours we took the local bus for shopping and to use facilities in Haifa. There was a cinema, where all the films had subtitles. There were several bars and enterprising restauranteurs who provided firm favourites like eggs or beans on toast. These were popular haunts which made a change from army food.

The prostitutes of many nationalities had their quarters there too, but they were obliged to ply their trade under strict medical regulations.

In August 1941 when training was completed, our platoon members were split up amongst various other regiments. I was posted to the Second Royal Horse Artillery unit in Giza, near Cairo and the pyramids. Several regiments camped there in the blazing heat under canvas.

CHAPTER FIVE
ACTION

Never had I experienced such intense heat as that at Giza. The hectic days began with reveille at 6.00am. We were obliged to retire to shade, exhausted at lunchtime, and resume duties later in the afternoons.

One of my first tasks was to paint blue and white serial letters and numbers onto new boards to be attached to the fronts of our regimental trucks. I was informed the original ones had been 'lost' in action during battles fought in Crete.

Additional 'bull' was enforced at Giza regarding laundry, of which I disapproved. It concerned the epaulettes on army shirts. They had to be stiffened, requiring more starch. We were compensated with a few more pence in our pay packets, but it was a reprimand for any soldier caught out with limp epaulettes.

The regime in the Royal Horse Artillery was decidedly brutal for offenders found guilty of insubordination or misdemeanours such as absenting themselves without leave (AWOL).

Soldiers placed on jankers were forced at gunpoint to run up and down a very steep manmade gradient in full battledress and pack in the searing tropical heat. Simply to witness the punishment was torture and a sufficient deterrent to others to abide by the rules.

I was authorised to take an intensive driving course, reluctantly initially, but was later appreciative for the opportunity to broaden my career prospects. The main road at Giza ran parallel with the River Nile, so extreme caution was required. One false move and I could so easily have been down the embankment and in it.

During off duty evenings, while learning to drive, under supervision of course, I was allowed to transport a load of mates down to the clubs and sometimes to the ENSA shows in Cairo.

The buzzing bazaars there were always so lively; heaving with bodies and a variety of interesting activities. I was fascinated by the continuous hammering and the creative objects produced from open forges in the metal workshops. I used to watch decorative plaques and utensils appear as if by magic from metal sheeting.

White-clad, aged Arabs with leathery, crinkled complexions crouched outside entrances to most of the shops, smoking their traditional 'Hubbly Bubblies'. These were strange-looking large glass jars, with long rubber pipes attached to the mouthpieces.

I found Cairo exceptionally noisy, a complete contrast to my own quiet village and local towns in England. There was incessant shouting and chatting as people bartered for goods at the markets. The metallic racket from the clanking, old, single-deck trams signalled their arrival as they rattled along the twisting tracks. They were open to the elements and it was a common occurrence for passengers, mainly soldiers, to lean out of the window spaces to take fruit from carts alongside. The owners shouted abuse adding more excitement to the hurly burly. I was entitled to a week's leave whilst stationed at Giza. My mate Harold Leutchford and I eagerly anticipated a welcome break at the army's expense at Fenham barracks in Cairo.

The barracks looked very impressive. They were built around a spacious, square, cream, ceramic-tiled courtyard. Overlooking balconies housed mattresses on the floor where we slept, or were supposed to sleep. Unfortunately for us, they were severely infested with bed bugs and we were nearly bitten to death. After two nights of torture and suffering through lack of sleep, we decided to abandon the holiday and return to camp to recover. Not before making our grievances felt at Fenham.

The remainder of the week we spent relaxing and socialising, by which time our regiment was preparing for action in the desert to relieve the Fourth Indian Division which we actually passed as they returned to Cairo.

We were to act as reinforcements for the Scots Guards, the Infantry, Tank and Anti-Tank Regiments. The Royal Corp of Signals were attached to our platoon.

In convoy we had sixteen twenty-five pounder Howitzer guns, four to each battery with twenty personnel. Our lorries were Canadian Chevrolets. When we arrived at our destination, we camped behind our firing lines.

We were with Headquarters and it was our specific duty to ensure that emergency supplies of petrol and food, delivered to us by the Royal Ordnance Corps, reached the front. Each night we bivouacked two to a tent. A split mosquito net covered the entrance to exclude the huge black flies which plagued us mercilessly.

They came in their trillions, from where? What did they live on? I never knew. The intense dry heat was certainly conducive to their breeding cycle. I had to be quick and careful when eating anything, otherwise I would get a mouthful. I couldn't write letters, they attacked the paper. The only relief came in the cool evenings when the majority of them retreated temporarily.

I made numerous treacle traps from empty petrol cans and caught millions, but relentlessly they came. It was common practice to fire the traps under cover of darkness but then the process would begin all over again with a vengeance at daybreak.

The petrol was delivered in wooden boxes, two four gallon cans to each box. I thought the wood packaging would be most useful. I knocked out two sides from two boxes, and cut a semi-circle in each one with a machete. When the two were joined together and well sandpapered, it made a utility toilet seat. However crude, it was certainly more sophisticated and comfortable than the usual routine in the desert. I made quite a few more as they proved very popular and portable, but a spade was still required.

Gazelles roamed freely beyond our encampment. Our Regimental Sergeant Major often asked me to drive him out into the desert to search for fresh meat. He was a crack shot with a rifle and we rarely returned without a carcass. It wasn't all fun; one day I suffered a severe reprimand through no fault of my own. We were travelling over stony, sandy territory and the track was very uneven. Just as my RSM had prey in his sights and was about to shoot, the Chevrolet bounced off an extremely undulating knoll. It caught him off balance and he missed his target.

Succulent gazelle meat tasted like fresh beef, adding a touch of luxury to our menu. It was appreciated as a welcome change to the corned beef we had been served in a variety of concoctions as our staple diet.

One of the lads said he had eaten so much “bully” that if he heard a whip crack he would start a stampede. We all agreed wholeheartedly but at least it was food.

One day the cook slipped up, accidentally putting salt in the rice pudding instead of sugar. I bet his ears were burning. Most of us ate it because there was no alternative. Fortunately we had a good water supply at that time, because it made us very thirsty.

Since leaving Cairo, it was my specific duty to be the driver for our intelligence officer. His equipment included a variety of maps to assist with his tasks. As our troops advanced, the Signals Corp sent enemy base grid reference numbers to our Royal Air Force bombers several miles to our rear.

Bombing raids were regular occurrences but we were also in great danger from our own aeroplanes, because as the enemy retreated, we advanced and their grid references became ours.

It was September and it had been heavy going for three weeks. We had been under constant pressure taking supplies to the front.

Suddenly orders came through for us to retreat. Our observation post officer had witnessed the German advancement.

When my orders came, the Chevrolet wouldn't start; the battery was shorting. Time was precious and it was reluctantly abandoned. I hitched a lift on one of our other wagons to retreat a few miles to a safer position.

After we re-camped, our deliveries began again. It became a waiting game with the atmosphere at this stage very tense. We didn't know how far forward the Germans had pushed.

Our intelligence officers and men in the Signals Corps were working to capacity under extreme conditions to get messages through. No one could underestimate or anticipate German strategies at this time.

The emergency camp covered a wide area. It was in a tight circular formation, with provisions and supplies occupying the central area. Around the perimeter were guard tanks, anti-tanks, Honey tanks and Infantry, so that if we were attacked we could retaliate and defend. The American Honey tanks, forming part of the Armoured Division, differed from the Matildas in that they were much smaller, nippier, and had rubber tracks instead of the characteristic caterpillar treads. They caused much devastation to superior German guns and equipment, discharging lethal shells under cover of darkness as they darted in and out of enemy danger zones at incredible speeds.

The only disadvantage of the Honey tanks was acquisition of spares. A second tank had to be immobilised before it could be cannibalised for replacement parts.

Continuous watch against surprise attacks was essential, especially during hours of darkness. Luckily for us, none came. A calm but apprehensive atmosphere prevailed for a few days.

Since the fighting had ceased temporarily, Harold and I were granted a few days outstanding leave. Although we had no transport, we had access to supply wagons, so we hitched a lift to Cairo.

We stayed at the Strand Hotel, which had been commandeered by the British Army. It was a pleasant relief to soak up the relaxed atmosphere away from the stressful action at the front.

Haifa - Jack bottom right

Harold and I made the most of the places of entertainment and the local bars. I had my photograph taken wearing an Egyptian Fez, to include in my next letter home.

We had to use our initiative to return to base camp as there was no transport available. If we failed to contact our platoon we were authorised to report to any tank regiment as gunners. This option didn't appeal to me, I preferred my own regiment.

Harold and I questioned all personnel in supply wagons until we

Cairo

encountered some returning to the front in our direction. We were lucky to hitch a ride back with reinforcements.

During our absence in the slight lull, the regiments had regrouped and reorganised.

Shortly after our return, heavy bombardment began again with a vengeance. The constant pounding of gunfire was continuous with casualties on both sides. The hot air was saturated with the acrid odour of gunpowder and curling clouds of dense, grey smoke was visible for miles. Well up front were the courageous infantry, covered by gallant gun crews, firing volleys over their heads at enemy targets, using grid references supplied by daring observation post officers.

The soldiers manning the anti-tank guns and twenty-five pounder Howitzers were slaving in the midst of hostilities, desperately fighting for their lives, kin and country.

Our superiors warned us that if we heard whistling sounds to disregard them - they were only shells flying over - but if the gunfire sounded closer to take cover immediately, which we generally did. It was impossible to anticipate where shells would land and explode. I only hoped and prayed there wasn't one with my name on.

We lost several supply wagons, and the black tell-tale smoke served as signals to the enemy that they were bang on target.

It was catastrophic when ammunition wagons were shelled. Their lethal contents exploded in all directions creating wanton havoc.

Fortunately, the Royal Army Medical Corp were always in attendance and our Brigadier was in continuous radio contact with all other regiments. It wasn't just the human element experiencing intense pressure from close range combat, the twenty-five pounder gun barrels had distorted with constant use and required replacements. Our equipment and wagons were in dire need of maintenance work too. This was the responsibility of the Royal Electrical and Mechanical Engineers.

November 1941

We received orders to pull back. Our positions were replaced by field artillery, as our platoon withdrew several miles and halted close to the coast of Rackham Bay. It was a pleasant opportunity to recuperate from battle fatigue, while our wagons were repaired.

Even though it was November, it was very sunny and warm

during the day and I enjoyed a couple of peaceful weeks, especially soaking up the balmy, fresh air and bathing in the luxurious, blue Mediterranean. What spoilt the holiday and what I detested, were the huge, black, nocturnal sand beetles, which descended upon us in droves. They were much bigger than any I had ever seen in England. It intrigued me as to how they grew to such proportions and what they ate. The area was a vast wilderness until our arrival, with only occasional clumps of tufty grass palms. There was nothing obvious for them to feed on. They emitted humming and purring sounds, which signalled their presence and disturbed our sleep. The mere thoughts of these unpleasant creatures crawling over my face as I slept made me squirm. They always appeared to surface under my kit bag pillow. The evening routines there followed the same patterns, beginning with searches under the groundsheets and blankets, and attempts to brush the invading beetles outside the tents.

It was back to battle when the repairs to our transport and equipment had been completed. We regrouped and returned to join the other regiments in the firing lines, who were deep in the midst of heavy engagements with the enemy. My duties continued: transporting essential supplies.

One of our observation post officers was Officer Quillian and his driver was Gunner Bentley. They used a fifteen hundredweight Morris wagon for their reconnaissance activities. It had been stripped down to its bare essentials by men from REME. Anything weighty and surplus to requirements, the spare wheel, hood, rear seats and rifle brackets had been removed, to enhance speed if a hasty retreat was necessary. Quillian and Bentley had the intelligence reconnoitring job down to a fine art, until eventually the inevitable happened. One day, they failed to return. Regretfully, we heard they had been captured. They were exceedingly brave men, who had often laughed at their daring escapades, dismissing them as trivial. I began to wonder who would be next.

Our infantry advanced steadily. Fighting was conducted from narrow, shallow trenches to give ground cover because the approaching shells exploded horizontally upon impact.

Initially we had to dig our own trenches, but as we pushed forward we were able to utilise some of the enemy trenches.

As the Germans retreated, Italian soldiers often remained fighting the rear guard. It soon became apparent that they booby-trapped many of the trenches they vacated. We were authorised to be extra vigilant when advancing, but often there was insufficient time, especially when diving for cover during bombing raids.

We were also warned not to seek souvenirs. The tips or butts of enemy rifles protruding from the sand were sometimes attached to mines. It was traumatic to witness or hear of any of our lads who lost their lives in this manner.

Mid-December 1941

During our advancement, we discovered a German half-track gun vehicle, which presumably had been knocked out of action by our artillery. Its engine was still running even though five German operators had all been killed outright.

Following the conventions of war, it was our responsibility to bury the dead. Their identity documents were removed and handed over to our intelligence officer.

We placed the uniformed bodies in shallow trenches, covered them and left their characteristic helmets on top. After immobilising their vehicle to render it useless for further warfare, should circumstances change, we continued to advance slowly under heavy shellfire. This was the pattern throughout December.

There were no opportunities for seasonal festivities. Naturally at this time of year, all thoughts were back home with loved ones, mine were no exception, especially since it was my second Christmas in the army.

It was a complete contrast to last year's festivities in training at Marske by the Sea when following tradition, the officers waited on the lower ranks for Christmas lunch. I couldn't help wondering how they were all faring in England, especially my family and friends; how they were celebrating Christmas and if it was snowing.

I didn't know where our Bob and Bill's regiments were stationed, but I hoped their conditions were better than ours and that they were safe and well.

Our Christmas fare was the usual bully beef hash with rice and we were grateful for it. I received my one and only card from Mum and Dad, it had a picture of a boat on the front. I propped it on the dashboard of our Chevrolet as a seasonal reminder. It directed my thoughts away from this dreadful wanton destruction.

There were no Christmas presents or food parcels for any of us. We were known as the Middle East Forces, we dubbed ourselves the MEF - the Men England Forgot.

War Graves, Libya

Libya

Although we were all aware of combat conditions in our immediate locality, we were vague about circumstances in other areas. I felt we were deliberately kept very much in the dark about the war throughout the rest of Europe for propaganda purposes.

As far as I was concerned from my limited experiences, it was touch and go, and it could go either way. Though at the back of my mind I always felt we had the edge.

Rommel and his Africa Korp were just ahead as we continued to maintain our positions.

CHAPTER SIX
CAPTURE

28th December 1941

It was just another routine delivery day for us. Our convoy had received orders to take supplies of food and petrol to the new North African base at Ajdabiyah in Libya, for the British troops' advancement there.

At 7.45am our intelligence officer returned from reconnoitring in the sand dunes and escarpments ahead. He gave us the assurance that the route we were to take was clear. Through his binoculars he had only seen a camel train.

This was quite a common sighting, many Bedouin tribes camped in black tents in the desert and were often spotted on our right flank, close to the coast. They didn't appear to get involved in any fighting, but I was always suspicious and didn't trust them.

I remembered the time of our retreat in September and thought some of them may have been responsible for reporting our positions to German intelligence.

We later realised what our officer thought was a camel train must either have been masking, or actually was, a German Panzer division of six half-track gun vehicles. They were operated by Hitler's trigger-happy youth army, and unobserved, had encircled the right flank of our firing line. Their presence had been concealed by the dunes. Suddenly they appeared behind us, isolating ten of our wagons from the main convoy.

We were surrounded as they fired warning shots into the air. We had no alternative but to stop and quickly jump for cover. The safest place, if there was one, appeared to be behind a wheel. There was no opportunity to defend or retaliate. we only had our rifles, which were useless against their half-track anti-tank guns.

The situation was critical, the atmosphere chilling, even so it didn't prevent one of our men, a sergeant from the Twelfth Lancers, firing his rifle and instantly killing the officer in charge.

"My God, we're for it now," I whispered almost involuntarily. They could have blasted the lot of us to Kingdom Come, however, in this instance luck was on our side. From a German point of view it may have been difficult to prove who had actually fired the fatal shot, but there were no reprisals. They appeared to be more interested in our supplies and capture.

There were forty of us. We were rounded up at gunpoint, our weapons confiscated and the wagons commandeered. We were captives.

"This is it," I thought. My brain was in turmoil, racing ahead to sinister stories I'd heard about interrogation tactics.

I quickly removed my regimental cap badge of the Royal Horse Artillery and buried it in the sand. "They are not going to find out which regiment I belong to, or anything about any troop movements from me." I muttered under my breath.

Some of us had to lie on top of the stacks of four gallon petrol cans in our own wagons. There were five hundred gallons in all. The remaining British men were forced to drive the wagons at gunpoint with Germans sitting in the front of the cabs. Their gun carriage was at the rear with the barrel aimed at the back of the convoy.

We then followed the same route the Germans had used to capture us and were soon in enemy territory, in range of our own firing lines. A very daunting situation indeed as we found ourselves en-route to Rommel's Headquarters near Ajdabiyah.

The journey only took half an hour, but because our wagons were sheeted with thick canvas, some of the men on top of the petrol cans were overcome by fumes. We quickly pulled them to the rear of the wagon nearer the fresh air to recover.

At headquarters, Rommel and his aides stood before us, while our wagons were driven off. He was a tall, well-built, imposing character who looked most impressive in his pristine uniform, peaked cap and goggles. He was recognised on both sides as one of the best German Commanders, remarkably cunning and aptly nicknamed the Desert Fox. He didn't appear to be interested in us only our invaluable fuel, provisions and wagons.

After a brief conversation with his officers Rommel returned to his quarters while one of them came towards us. In impeccable English he said, as he tapped each one of us on the shoulder,

"For you the war is over. I feel very sorry for you. You see, you are captured on Italian territory, therefore we are obliged to hand you over to the Italian Authorities. They are themselves so poor, they have nothing for you."

With that he clicked his heels, about turned and marched off.

"Phew! What next?" was the burning question as we eagerly began to light up cigarettes. I took out my army booklet AB64 where my occupation at conscription was listed as 'coal bagger'. With my cigarette, I very carefully burnt out coal bagger and inserted 'joiner' in the space above. I turned to my mate and said, "They're not getting me down any bloody German coalmine."
Italian armed guards then closed in, demanding to search us. We were forced to empty our pockets on the sand where we stood. They rummaged through our personal possessions. I had a small canvas satchel attached to my belt containing mine. They took it and the contents. The amazing thing was, they only kept the articles they particularly wanted. We were allowed to keep jewellery, watches, letters, notes, photographs and toiletries, such as razors and combs. Unfortunately, they confiscated lighters and all our cigarettes. That was disastrous since only the previous day

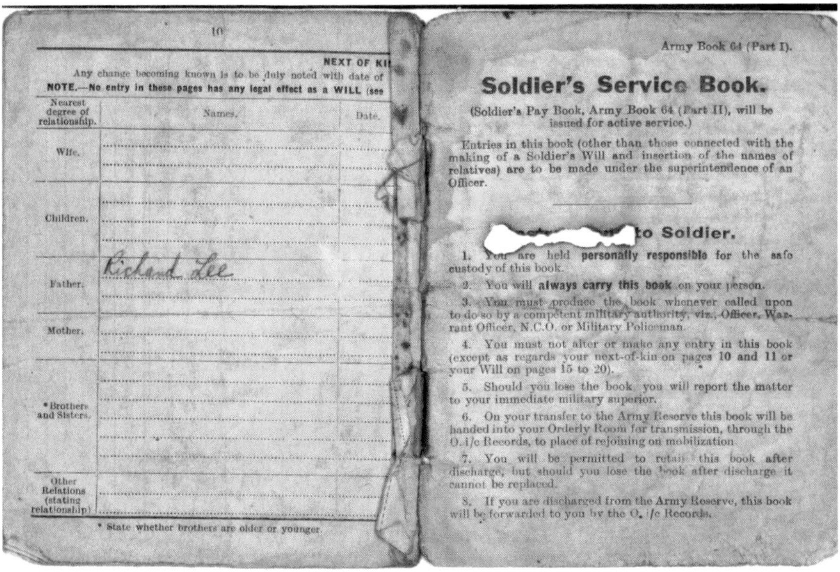

10

NEXT OF KI

Any change becoming known is to be duly noted with date of

NOTE.—No entry in these pages has any legal effect as a WILL (see

Nearest degree of relationship.	Names.	Date.
Wife.		
Children.		
Father.	Richard Lee	
Mother.		
*Brothers and Sisters.		
Other Relations (stating relationship)		

* State whether brothers are older or younger.

Army Book 64 (Part I).

Soldier's Service Book.

(Soldier's Pay Book, Army Book 64 (Part II), will be issued for active service.)

Entries in this book (other than those connected with the making of a Soldier's Will and insertion of the names of relatives) are to be made under the superintendence of an Officer.

[illegible] to Soldier.

1. [illegible] are held **personally responsible** for the safe custody of this book.
2. You will **always carry this book** on your person.
3. You must produce the book whenever called upon to do so by a competent military authority, viz., Officer, Warrant Officer, N.C.O. or Military Policeman.
4. You must not alter or make any entry in this book (except as regards your next-of-kin on pages 10 and 11 or your Will on pages 15 to 20).
5. Should you lose the book you will report the matter to your immediate military superior.
6. On your transfer to the Army Reserve this book will be handed into your Orderly Room for transmission, through the O. i/c Records, to place of rejoining on mobilization.
7. You will be permitted to retain this book after discharge, but should you lose the book after discharge it cannot be replaced.
8. If you are discharged from the Army Reserve, this book will be forwarded to you by the O. i/c Records.

Soldier's Service Book

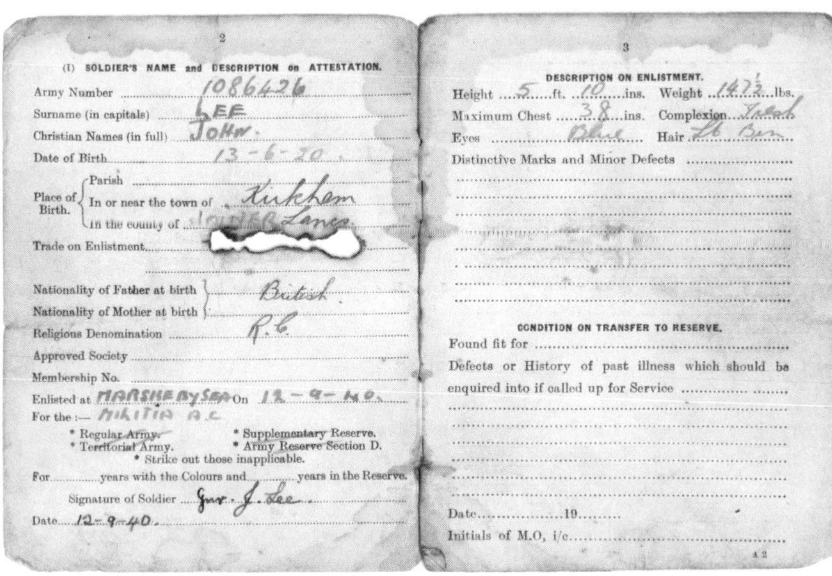

2

(I) SOLDIER'S NAME and DESCRIPTION on ATTESTATION.

Army Number 1086426
Surname (in capitals) LEE
Christian Names (in full) JOHN.
Date of Birth 13-6-20.
Place of Birth. Parish
In or near the town of Kirkham
In the county of [illegible] Lancs
Trade on Enlistment [illegible]
Nationality of Father at birth / Nationality of Mother at birth British.
Religious Denomination R.C.
Approved Society
Membership No.
Enlisted at MARSKE BY SEA On 12-9-40.
For the :— MILITIA A.C
* Regular Army. * Supplementary Reserve.
* Territorial Army. * Army Reserve Section D.
* Strike out those inapplicable.
For .... years with the Colours and .... years in the Reserve.
Signature of Soldier Jno. J. Lee.
Date 12-9-40.

3

DESCRIPTION ON ENLISTMENT.

Height 5 ft. 10 ins. Weight 147½ lbs.
Maximum Chest 38 ins. Complexion Fresh
Eyes Blue Hair Lt Brn
Distinctive Marks and Minor Defects

CONDITION ON TRANSFER TO RESERVE.

Found fit for
Defects or History of past illness which should be enquired into if called up for Service
Date .... 19........
Initials of M.O, i/c ....

A 2

Shows word 'Joiner' over burnt section of book

we had received our weekly issue and were consequently well-stocked.

It was a double blow for me to lose my barber's tools, I'd had them since joining up, initially only for my own use, but then I began a short back and sides service in exchange for a few cigarettes. This meant they took double cigarettes from me.

When the search was over, we were kept outside for a few hours under armed guard. At least we were able to chat amongst ourselves, but the main topics of conversation were predictions regarding our destiny.

Two large Italian open wagons arrived. Twenty men to each, standing room only, under armed guard, and we were on our way to Italian Headquarters at Surte for interrogation.

We had completed roughly half the journey when suddenly out of the blue, our own Maryland bombers zoomed overhead bombing and strafing us because we had crossed into German firing lines. Pandemonium let loose, someone said "Scatter!" and we didn't hang about as we dispersed in all directions. One of our lads shouted, "Quick make a victory sign and then they'll know we're British."

We hurriedly lay down on the sand, in as large a V, head to toe, as our bodies permitted. Whether or not the pilots realised we were British I shall never know. Luckily for us, only two soldiers caught shrapnel in their tough army boots as the second burst descended. Both wagons received direct hits - exploding the petrol tanks and burning out.

Crisis over, the bombers flew back into the horizon, and we were rounded up. Huddled close together, we had no alternative but to sit and wait another two hours for replacement transport. The remainder of the journey was completed without incident and we were officially handed over to the Italian Authorities.

At Surte we were led behind a converted farmhouse building into what was previously a shippon. We were singled out for interrogation which took place in a smaller room.

I knew the rules: according to the Geneva Convention, give only rank, name and number. Before the interrogation began, the Italian Officer said, if we co-operated and gave them the information they required, they would supply us with food.

It was late afternoon and we hadn't eaten since breakfast, we were beginning to feel hungry and thirsty.

Morale was pretty low at this stage, due to the exceptional circumstances of the day, the distance we'd travelled, and the dry warmth of the afternoon even though it was December.

Eventually my turn came. At gunpoint I was led into the small, sparsely-furnished room to be confronted by two formidable-looking Italian Officers seated behind a solid wooden table. I stood at ease as I was asked my name.

"Jack Lee."

"Rank?"

"Gunner."

"Number?"

"1086426."

In very precise English came the next question. "What can you tell us of any movements behind your lines?"

"I know nothing," to which one of the officers snapped,

"You must know something!"

"I said I know nothing and I mean I know nothing."

My dismissal came with the shout,

"Next!"

My own opinion was they were well-briefed and knew a darn sight more about our troop movements than we did.

The same pattern of interrogation continued until all forty of us had seen the inside of the small room. I couldn't say the two Italian Officers were aggressive, but they were quite shirty they hadn't discovered any new information.

Two more Italian soldiers appeared carrying cardboard boxes from which we each received a small tin of processed meat similar to 'Spam.' There was no label or indication of its source of origin. We also received a small concrete like biscuit about three inches square.

I didn't particularly enjoy the food, but survival was the name of the game, so I ate it all. Two different Italian wagons were outside waiting to take us on the next stage of the journey. Throughout the night we travelled. Sleep evaded us because it was standing room only, propping each other up shoulder to shoulder. We began to feel dehydrated, we'd had nothing to drink for over 24 hours and we were very hungry and feverishly cold.

It was one of the longest nights of my entire life. I saw the sun rise through bleary eyes long before we reached our destination, which was an ex-Italian army barracks at Tarhunah.

There were buildings on both sides of the square, with a wire perimeter fence to the front and rear. The barrack room was spacious and devoid of furnishings. We each received a small cup of lukewarm black coffee without sugar, this was breakfast. Then we were issued with one grey army blanket and a straw mat on which we were to sit or sleep.

Lunch at midday consisted of a small ladle of boiled macaroni or rice, barely flavoured with tomato or cheese, served in a kidney shaped dixie. There was no choice, it was macaroni one day, rice the next, and that was it. There was nothing else for the remainder of the day.

On our second day at Tarhunah, the Italian Officer in charge took us all outside into a small compound. We were ordered to have our hair sheared off. A few of the lads didn't mind, the ones who had crew cuts previously, but for the majority of us it was a direct infringement of personal liberties.

The officer said it was for hygienic reasons, the guards carried rifles, we had no alternative but to accept the orders.

It was very difficult to sleep at Tarhunah. We soon began to suffer pressure point pains in our backs and buttocks from the straw mats on the hard, red, ceramic floor. The tiles remained cool during the daytime and were perishing cold at night. During the hours of wakefulness, we also began to suffer the griping pains of intense hunger. The starvation diet was a form of torture, as weight visibly fell away from our bodies in such a short time.

We began to barter with the guards, anything we could for a piece of bread, or a bun. I parted company with my treasured wrist watch, just for a small amount of bread. I could only eat a tiny portion at a time, my stomach had shrunk so much. I knew from experience, seeing the other lads sick, it would make me ill. The bread kept me going for twenty-four hours, then the hunger pains began again. Many of the men traded their most valuable possessions, such as wedding rings and jewellery, for food.

During the morning of our second day at Tarhunah, an Italian officer randomly selected a few of our men for work. It was in an ordnance type factory building at the far end of the compound. Spare parts for motors and tanks were stored there awaiting packaging and dispatching to the various German army bases throughout the desert.

The same routine was followed each morning, so that eventually everybody in turn had an opportunity to experience the work. The first men to return told us what they had done. To them the 'work' consisted of causing as much sabotage as was humanely possible without the threat of discovery. Thereafter it became a game, which when reporting back, gave us our only kicks.

Many small, vital, movable parts, such as nuts, bolts and petrol can caps, were removed inconspicuously and disposed of in the adjacent fields. The petrol cans were rendered useless by puncturing them with minute holes.

During the few weeks we stayed at Tarhunah, our activities at the ordnance depot were never rumbled. No doubt those fighting men in the desert at the receiving end of each consignment, cursed the inadequacy of their stores department. We sincerely hoped so.

Many plots to escape were planned, but couldn't be put into practice due to shortage of food. The Italians kept several pigs behind the ordnance factory. Some of our men looked after them, but only so that they could pick up and eat scraps of food fed to the pigs. We were all so desperately hungry.

When not 'working' there was nothing we could do. We lounged about and chatted amongst ourselves, heavily guarded. Time dragged so much, we were relieved to hear we were to be on the move again.

We were bound for Tripoli, transported by army trucks to the picturesque harbour, where the Italian destroyer which was to be our escort was anchored off shore. My heart sank when I saw our craft. It was the most decrepit old cargo boat I had ever seen. Could this heap of scrap be seaworthy, I wondered? We were hustled down into the dark depths of the hold. The black timbers were saturated, giving off a dank, musty stench.

There was no opportunity to escape; armed Italian soldiers guarded the deck. The final misery came when the hatch was battened down.

When we were a few miles out at sea, we began to list heavily. More water seeped through and began to slurp about alarmingly underfoot. We fell about like nine-pins. The swell was horrendous, we were panic-stricken and convinced we were to share a watery grave. The captain of the destroyer must have thought the same, because he ordered our captors back to Tripoli.

The pitching and rolling eased once back in calmer waters, much to my relief. I wasn't surprised to discover the barge had previously been holed. On land we staggered about like drunkards with jelly legs, our muscles weak, barely able to support us.

Primitive Italian ambulances arrived to take us to Trig-Tarhunah, an army fortification. Only a small area of the roof was visible, most of the building was concealed below ground level, well-camouflaged with grass. It was like stepping into an ancient stone dungeon. I experienced an icy chill as I crossed the threshold. The room was circular with whitened walls. Presumably to reflect the little light available from occasional narrow slits near the ceiling, supplemented with a few dull electric lightbulbs. Continuous stone slabs circled the interior walls, these were our seats and beds. It was extremely cold, especially at night without blankets. The only protection against the stark, damp atmosphere were the clothes we wore. Everything was bleak, there was little for us to see or do but sit and wait, chat amongst ourselves, and wonder what was to come next.

We received the same meagre rations as those at Tarhunah. One cup of black coffee for breakfast and a ladle of macaroni for lunch. Although we had access to primitive toilets, there were no washing or shaving facilities. There was only one entrance to the fort. We were kept under guard, holed up for a week, by which time we all looked hairy and haggard. On the seventh day we were led out, dazed and startled by the intensity of the light, but thankful for the warmer temperature and fresh air.

Under armed escort we were transported back to Tripoli Harbour in the same antiquated ambulances. At gunpoint, we were forced aboard a different, ramshackled, old cargo craft, but at least this one was dry. We were herded into the hold like animals, but on this occasion the hatches were left open. A few of us were able to climb the ladders to listen and observe the situation on deck.

Apparently, Naples was to be our port of call, en-route to a further transit camp inland. The stretch of water was notoriously dangerous, not only from the underwater currents, but also because our British Naval submarines patrolled the depths. The Italian guards said many boats carrying British prisoners had been sunk by torpedoes, as if we didn't have enough problems to worry about.

During the voyage, morale hit rock bottom. Casually in the course of conversation, one chap suggested a mutiny. There followed a deadly hush, and we could almost sense the grey cells rapidly charging. We were from a varied range of occupations and ranks including wireless operators, infantry, gunners, medics and electricians. Feverishly the excited chattering began and spirits were uplifted with rebellious fervour. Several plots and strategies emerged, tactics were debated until the final plan was formulated. We would take over the vessel, starting with the signal room to get a message through to our Navy. Unfortunately, we didn't get the opportunity to put our plans into practice because time was against us, but at least the adrenalin was flowing.

After a twenty-two hour crossing we disembarked at Naples absolutely ravenous. We were each issued with a small tin of meat resembling streaky leather and a hard biscuit, before boarding a goods train to a transit camp at Capua. We were promised more food if we hurried. They were lies, all lies, there was no more food.

CHAPTER SEVEN
INTERNMENT – CAPUA, SERVIGLIANO

It was February the 11th 1942 when we arrived at Capua. We were grateful for the same meagre food previous camps had supplied and ate eagerly. We had no idea how long we were to remain at Capua and couldn't begin to anticipate conditions or consequences.

I was issued with four studded waterproof groundsheets which proved versatile. One could be used as a cape and six sheets made a tent so we all paired up. We were also given duck-boards - a type of palette, used as a foundation on the ground to support a straw mattress.

It was raining heavily when we arrived. The field to which we were directed was waterlogged. It soon became obvious why we needed duck-boards; to float the mattresses.

Many comrades were very sick at Capua, many more soon became violently ill and died. It was a very distressing place. I was one of the unfortunate ones who contacted dysentery. It was hardly surprising, apart from the appalling conditions, my resistance to infection must have been so low with a diet barely sufficient to sustain me.

I knew I was very ill. I literally crawled from my tent to report to the Italian Medical Officer in the barracks. My weight had dropped to seven stone. I was too weak to stand or walk. I joined the end of the queue and sat on the wooden floor, gradually inching my way along on my bottom until it was my turn.

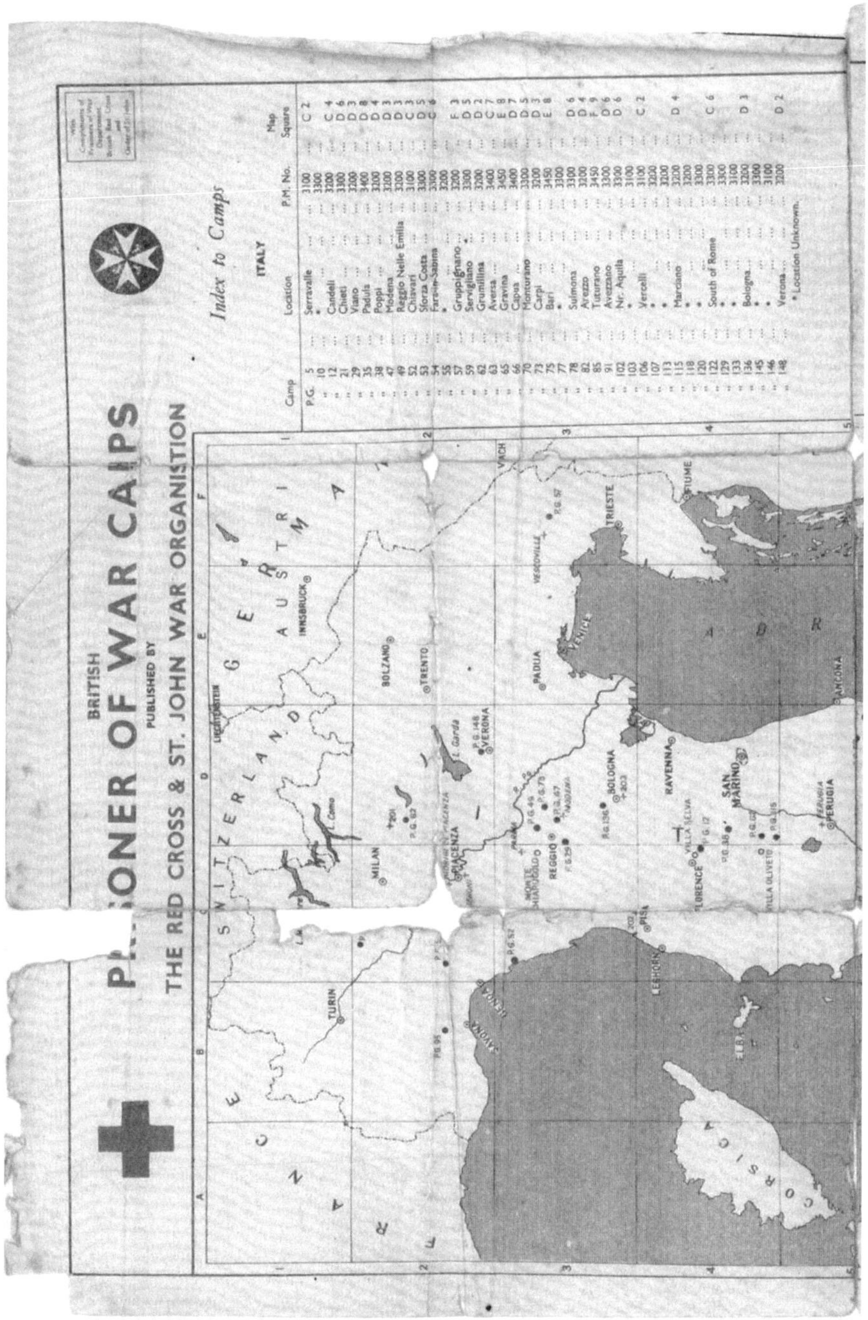

Prisoner of war camps Italy

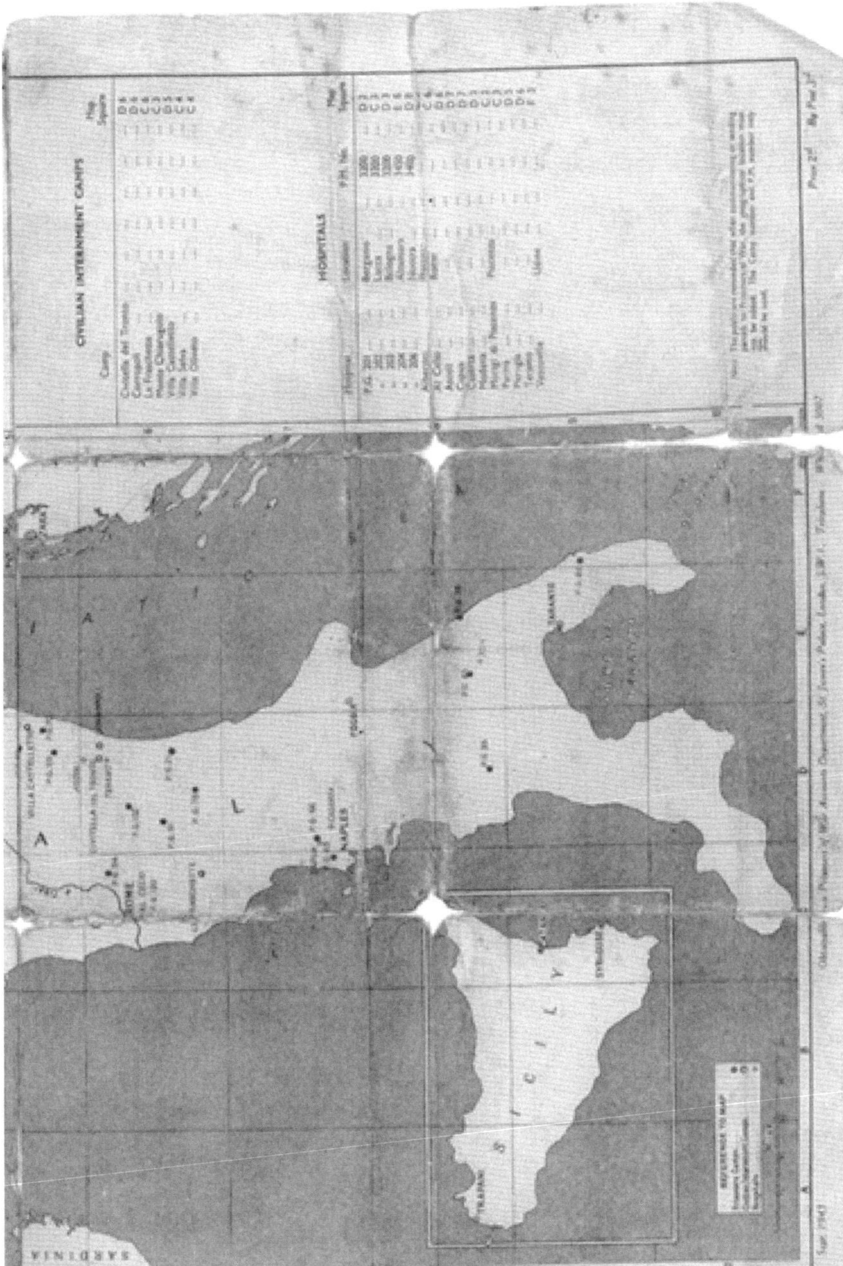

Prisoner of war camps Italy

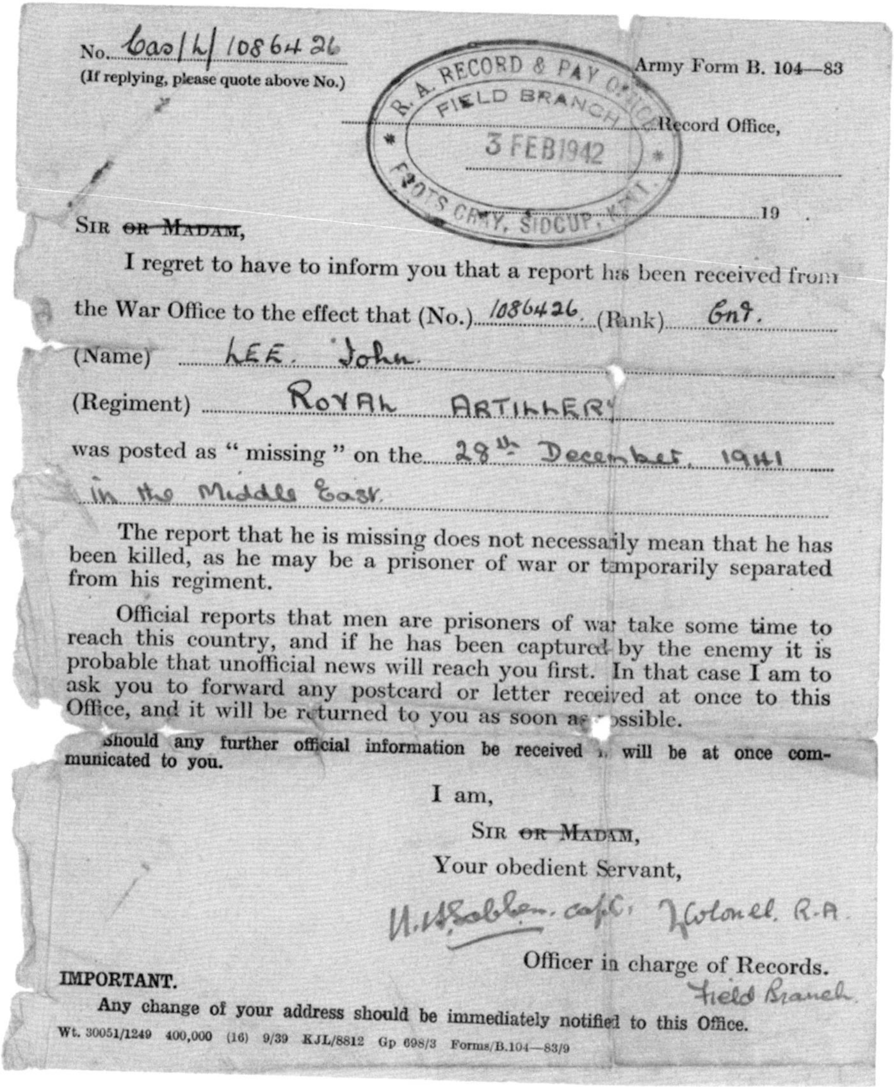

No. Cas/L/108626
(If replying, please quote above No.)

Army Form B. 104—83

Record Office,

19

SIR ~~OR MADAM~~,

I regret to have to inform you that a report has been received from the War Office to the effect that (No.) 108626 (Rank) Gnr.

(Name) LEE. John

(Regiment) ROYAL ARTILLERY

was posted as "missing" on the 28th December 1941 in the Middle East.

The report that he is missing does not necessarily mean that he has been killed, as he may be a prisoner of war or temporarily separated from his regiment.

Official reports that men are prisoners of war take some time to reach this country, and if he has been captured by the enemy it is probable that unofficial news will reach you first. In that case I am to ask you to forward any postcard or letter received at once to this Office, and it will be returned to you as soon as possible.

Should any further official information be received it will be at once communicated to you.

I am,

SIR ~~OR MADAM~~,

Your obedient Servant,

N. H. Sabben, cap. for Colonel. R.A.

Officer in charge of Records.
Field Branch

IMPORTANT.

Any change of your address should be immediately notified to this Office.

Wt. 30051/1249 400,000 (16) 9/39 KJL/8812 Gp 698/3 Forms/B.104—83/9

Posted 'missing letter' to parents

The Medical Officer took my temperature and gave me some M&B tablets. He told me I was to go to hospital before sending me back to bed. I could see the hospital building at the far end of the compound. There was no-one to help me back to my tent. I sat on the floor and the reverse process began, inch by inch in what appeared to be an eternity.

My mate was very poorly too, he lay motionless on his bed. When the ambulance eventually arrived to collect me, the Italians proceeded to place him on the stretcher, I stared in utter disbelief. I was so weak all I could say was,

"No, no, it's for me!"

"Nix, nix." was the response pointing to my colleague and quick as a flash, they had gone. I lay exhausted, the dratted disease had drained every last ounce of energy from my skeletal frame. I closed my eyes, memories of my happy childhood came into focus. I could feel the warmth of the summer sunshine, and smell the meat and potatoes cooking. My mother was there by the stove in the kitchen busily stirring the pans. I could hear Harry, Bob and Bill playing outside. I was swinging on the front gate, waiting to see my dad strolling up the road after a hard day at work.

"He's coming," I shouted, "he's coming."

That was the last I remember, before mercifully slipping into oblivion.

"He's coming, he's coming," the distant voice echoed.

"He's coming round, he's coming round, quick - a drink of water."

"Hello Jack, you've slept the clock round, you had us worried for a while," said Jones.

I have no doubt whatsoever, that I owe my life to the two

comrades in the adjacent tent who cared for me during my crisis. They took my mug and dixie for rations and fed me. Even so it was quite a while before I was well enough to fend for myself. It was the usual practice in all the camps, the authorities made internees responsible for the welfare of each other.

I was lucky, dysentery was the killing scourge at Capua. During that time the Red Cross Officials were actually checking living conditions. The Italian Authorities went to extremes to prevent them visiting our chronic quarters. However, ten days before we left Capua, ankle deep in water, we were re-housed in unfurnished, wooden barrack rooms.

It was a red letter day when I received my first Red Cross parcel. The contents were donated by the British people and distributed through Lisbon. There was such excitement, it was better than a birthday or Christmas - a real tonic.

The parcels were about fifteen inches long and eight or nine inches wide. They were extremely well packed with selected goodies, which were included mainly because of their vitamin or high nutritional value. I kept a record of mine which contained nineteen small packages (apart from the larger tins of biscuits and milk) as follows:-

1. A cylindrical tin of McVities biscuits
2. A tin of meat roll – 'Spam' type
3. A tin of corned beef
4. A tin of beans in tomato sauce
5. A tin of meat and vegetables
6. A tin of KLIM concentrated powdered milk (spelt backwards)
7. A packet of cheese
8. A small tin of lemon curd
9. A tin of mustard

10. Two bars of lump sugar
11. A packet of dripping
12. A packet of margarine
13. A packet of toffee
14. A bar of chocolate
15. A bar of washing soap
16. A box of sultanas
17. A quarter pound of tea
18. A tin of Ovaltine
19. A packet of porridge oats

As well as these treasures, I could also have either a tin of fifty cigarettes or the equivalent in long cut pipe tobacco.

Needless to say, after the distribution of food parcels morale rocketed. The barrack room took on the appearance of a noisy commercial market hall, as items were eagerly bartered to suit individual tastes and preferences.

I swapped my corned beef for porridge oats, because I had been brought up on it and one small packet would provide three or four meals.

The eyes of the Italian guards nearly popped out with envy when they saw all our luxuries. It reminded me of what the German officer had said at Ajdabiyah. It was true, they had nothing and were also suffering, but not as much as us.

The guards too exchanged cigarettes for food, forty for a tin of corned beef or a bar of soap. Even though Italian cigarettes were of poorer quality than British, they were better than nothing and could be further exchanged amongst ourselves.

Roughly a quarter of our soldiers were black South Africans. When food parcels were issued at Capua, all the white people received one each. South Africans could only have one parcel between two, which we all thought grossly unfair.

We were paid one lira a day (equivalent to one penny) but the South Africans had to share one lira amongst four, and decided to complain about the unfairness to the guards, who informed their superiors. The consequence was the Italian guards rounded up all the South Africans and sorted out the ringleaders. They were punished. Their hands were chained above their heads and they were fastened to a telegraph pole facing the blazing sun for the remainder of the day.

We were all saddened by the occasion, these men were exceptionally skilled soldiers and riflemen who had fought alongside us bravely. We all got the message, the incident was simply an example to us; there were no further complaints. Had it been white people tortured in this manner, I have no doubt that they would have suffered severe sunstroke.

A special train was laid on to transport us to Camp 59, Servigliano, which was situated in a valley of vineyards. We arrived in the mid-morning heat of the following day.

Our numbers there made two thousand internees from most regiments of the Army, Navy and Air Force. There were one hundred and forty four men to a unit, sub-divided into four smaller sections with a sergeant in charge of each. The camp was surrounded by a ten foot high brick wall. It was interspersed with sentry boxes mounted on wood platforms, level with the top of the wall. The sentry boxes, fitted with high-powered searchlights, were permanently manned. Two feet inside the wall was a slit trench, not very deep, but we were informed there would be no mercy should any of us attempt to place one foot in the trench because the guards had orders to shoot.

Coupons at Servigliano

There was a nightly curfew. Any movement after dark would be located by the searchlights and offenders shot without question.

Surrounding each barrack room, housing one hundred and forty four men, was a dug-out trench where we were authorised to remain if there should be an air raid. During my time at Servigliano this situation didn't arise.

I received the grand total of one lira a day, paid out every ten days, in the form of specially printed coupons. This type of payment was to avoid the use of Italian currency, especially in an escape situation. It could only be spent in the camp kiosk which was built into the perimeter wall. Ten pence didn't go very far, so I had to be selective in my choice of necessities. These usually included shaving soap, matches, jam and cheese - a rubbery type to slice. Even though it was tasteless, I thought it nutritional. If there was any money left, I bought a dixie full of vino costing two lira.

One day, one of our lads, a sprightly boxer from Liverpool, spent all his allowance on vino. He became aggressively drunk and lashed out at the first guard he saw. The guards in the high sentry would have shot him, but all his mates closed in to surround him, enabling him to escape to the security of the barracks. He hid between two soldiers having a kip, but the guards sought him out. Even though he was paralytic, they frogmarched him off. We never saw him again, he was branded troublesome and imprisoned elsewhere.

Two days after our arrival at Servigliano we were informed we were to have typhoid injections, to be administered by our own British Medical internees. I had always feared needles, and because I felt my resistance to infection was low, I had a mug of water ready on the floor by my bunk for when my turn came. Immediately after the injection I hurried back and almost passed out. We were all suffering, we had very little stamina or antibodies to cope with the necessary typhoid jab, but I felt the water revived me.

Boils were a problem too, due to malnutrition. There was no medication. They were treated by good mates who either cut out the core with scissors, or applied the neck of an empty bottle to extract it by suction. This operation was very effective, but if it was a neck boil it nearly pulled off the patient's head in the process.

There were eight wooden-framed bunks to a unit, four up and four down with about a yard of space between each frame. We slept on straw-filled mattresses on wooden laths. Our pillows were straw sandbags. With constant use, the straw gradually disintegrated and became solid.

There were thirteen laths to each bed frame. Some of the men decided they could manage with only twelve, chopping the thirteenth to use as fuel in makeshift stoves. These were constructed out in the exercise yard.

The Italian guards held random checks to count the laths. Anyone caught with less than the regulation number was immediately confined to the primitive brick built prison, with loss of privileges for a week.

Those on detention when Red Cross parcels were distributed missed out, but any personal parcels from home were kept until offenders were released.

It was the responsibility of the comrades of those under detention to obtain their food for them from the large, basic cook-house in the corner of the compound. Either macaroni or spaghetti was ladled from large, square metal containers by our own men.

From our Red Cross parcels, we always saved flat, Horlicks tablet tins. They were just the right size to hold five cigarettes and a few wax matches. The tin was filled and resealed with its own adhesive strip and concealed in the dixie under the macaroni or spaghetti so that confined mates were not totally deprived of their smokes.

It was several weeks before we actually received the first batch of Red Cross parcels at Servigliano. Excited rumours about their arrival circulated because they were delivered by rail and some of the lads put two and two together when they heard trains stop outside the camp. It was often our Deputy Camp Leader, I never knew his name, just called him Griff, who spread the news. He was a generous soul who had our wellbeing at heart. Much of his time was spent with the 'top brass' on both sides and through interpreters had access to 'classified' information. Griff delighted in discovering and supplying news items to keep our spirits high.

The wooden bed bunk frames were thoroughly contaminated with nasty bed bugs, causing discomfort and distress amongst us all. The brown-red beetle-type creatures as big as ladybirds were blood suckers. Apart from the irritating initial bites, the skin ballooned into blisters and often became severely infected with scratching, taking considerably longer to heal.

Each week we were issued with a hard, green block of washing soap, about one and a half inches square. We discovered we could mould it like putty. We then used it to fill in as many of the bug holes in the bed frames as we could find. It wasn't a cure but it appeared to ease the beastly bug situation considerably. One of our lads discovered the soap was highly inflammable, so we also used it to kindle small fires for brewing up and cooking, saving Red Cross quality soap for personal use.

The cook-house internees used trees felled locally and brought in daily for cooking fuel. The bark which fell off during sawing was thrown over the fence into our compound. We were able to utilise this for personal cooking, but smaller branches we were obliged to purchase using our penny a day allowance. There was a scarcity of wood for individual needs, all Red Cross boxes or cardboard packages were available as fuel.

Tobacco supplies issued to prisoners resembled ready rubbed, but it was ghastly stuff to smoke. We boiled it in tins to extract the nicotine, then used the solution to pour into the cracks and joints in our bed frames. This also proved an effective remedy against the evil bed bugs.

Each morning we were roused by bugle call at 8.00am. Breakfast consisted of only a small cup of black coffee, but supplemented with general provisions from Red Cross parcels.

Lunch was the small standard ladle of macaroni cheese or spaghetti, sometimes in tomato sauce. Occasionally there was a fennel, a vegetable similar to a white lettuce, or if we were very lucky, an orange. I understood these luxuries were procured with the money our British Government provided, which was one penny per day per man, but they were few and far between.

The evening meal was consistent; a bread roll with cheese about the size of a small matchbox, or on alternate days a small piece of meat. I called it 'mule' because it wouldn't go anywhere. It was tough, gristly and most unpalatable. More often than not I swapped my meat for cheese.

The cheese, although hard, was reasonably tasty. It was easy to grate on our home made kitchen-ware; tin lids perforated with nail holes. It could then be made into a spreading paste by mixing with a little freshly brewed, hot strong tea. I found the tea enhanced the flavour and made the cheese go a bit further.

We never ever discarded orange peel. Some men ate it, some used it to keep tobacco moist, but most of all it was dried and used as a fire lighter.

The procedure for handing out food parcels was different to that at Capua. There was no discrimination, all internees were treated equally. We were led in sections, thirty-six men at a time, to the distribution point. This was a serving hatch into a store room, built into and beyond the perimeter walls. A large stone flag covered the slit trench inside the wall and only one person at a time could approach the kiosk to receive a parcel.

Inside the store, the British Regimental Sergeant Major and an Italian officer presented the parcels which were passed up in line formation by several Italian soldiers. Again, we had the choice of a tin of fifty cigarettes or pipe tobacco. I always opted for cigarettes, and even non-smokers took their quota which could be bartered for food. Some unscrupulous prisoners punctured the bases of corned beef tins, heated them inside another recycled tin to extract the fat for culinary purposes, and then had the audacity to exchange the corned beef minus fat for other goods.

Most tin cans were salvaged for recycling. A flat pilchard tin could easily be converted into a small frying pan or plate. Some cans were used to make small forges or ovens. The cans were flattened and the seams joined by either hammering or with homemade rivets, similar to paper fasteners. The hammers were cobblestones we found within the compound.

The makeshift ovens were about seven inches square with a door at one end. These fit inside a larger tin box about nine inches square. The space between the two boxes was filled with earth which retained heat from an open fire or forge.

The forge consisted of two pulley wheels made from round biscuit tins, slotted together and connected to a powdered milk tin. This housed a flat tin fan on a wire shaft. It had a bobbin on the outside to take the pulley belts. A small rectangular cocoa tin was attached to the milk tin, to take the draught from the fan to the fire when the wire handle was turned.

The pulley belts were of canvas, from army issue trouser

braces. The bearings, where the shaft handle penetrated the tin were made from the leather part of the braces, joined with rivets.

The thick wire shaft and handle was extracted inconspicuously from the retaining fence at the far end of the compound. Some of the prisoners gifted with patience and ingenuity, made the bearings from army boot eyelets. One day, when I was making a forge fan box, a fellow from our section came towards me shouting, "That's my tin." He snatched it from me aggressively, almost severing two finger ends on my left hand.

Blood spurted out so profusely he backed off, while I legged it speedily to the medical hut. The doctor said I needed stitches, but he hadn't any. He said he could use black domestic sewing thread, but I refused. The only alternative was to secure the severed fingers with Elastoplast, which fortunately proved successful. The scarred skin remains and becomes white in cold weather.

The sergeant in charge of our unit reported any complaints we made back to our camp leader, Regimental Sergeant Major Peebles. He was a compassionate, elderly, tall, thin, gentleman.

He intervened on our behalf, when new battledresses arrived from the Ministry of Defence in England via the Red Cross. The Italians wanted to cut the sleeves of the tunics, to insert three inch bands of their dark blue uniform material. This was to make us more easily identifiable should any of us attempt to escape.

R.S.M. Peebles categorically refused to accept the battledresses if any of them were cut. Meanwhile the clothes we wore, the ones in which we were captured, were deteriorating rapidly and in dire need of replacement.

Some of the men who had been interned in other camps wore blue uniforms with khaki bands inserted in the right sleeves. It took a further two months to reach a compromise.

When I eventually received my new battledress, six inch

squares of bright red cotton material had been stitched onto the right shoulder panel of the tunic and the map pocket on the left side of the trousers. The patches were machined on so well with minute stitches, it would have been an impossible task to remove them without cutting the fabric. However, not to be outwitted, in typical "British Tommy", style and spirit, our men delighted in wiping their dirty hands and utensils on the patches so that they soon became less obvious.

My twenty-second birthday passed me by at Servigliano. As far as I was concerned there was nothing to celebrate, another year older, but years older in experiences I could have done without.

Six Italian women from the village washed our underclothes. They came into the camp every Thursday to collect it and to return the previous weeks' washing. I don't know what kind of soap they used but the garments always returned stiff as boards and very rough. If it was starch, they certainly weren't doing us any favours.

We experienced severe problems with lice at Servigliano, they appeared to invade and breed in the thick seams of the khaki battledress. Mine was steam-cleaned effectively twice by our own men. The lice were so disturbing some soldiers tried to burn or cut them out, inevitably many of the uniforms soon became tattered.

I had only one issue of new army boots at Servigliano. My old ones, even though well-worn, were recycled. The Italian residential army cobbler took off the heels from my old boots and attached three half-inch thick wads of leather to the soles; they made a good pair of utility football boots for me.

I played for the intercamp England team. Weekly fixtures were arranged amongst the four British Isles teams. We rarely finished a game to produce a final score because the Italian guards sounded the bugle to return to barracks before the end of the match. I regarded it as a petty reprisal, probably because our lads were all so

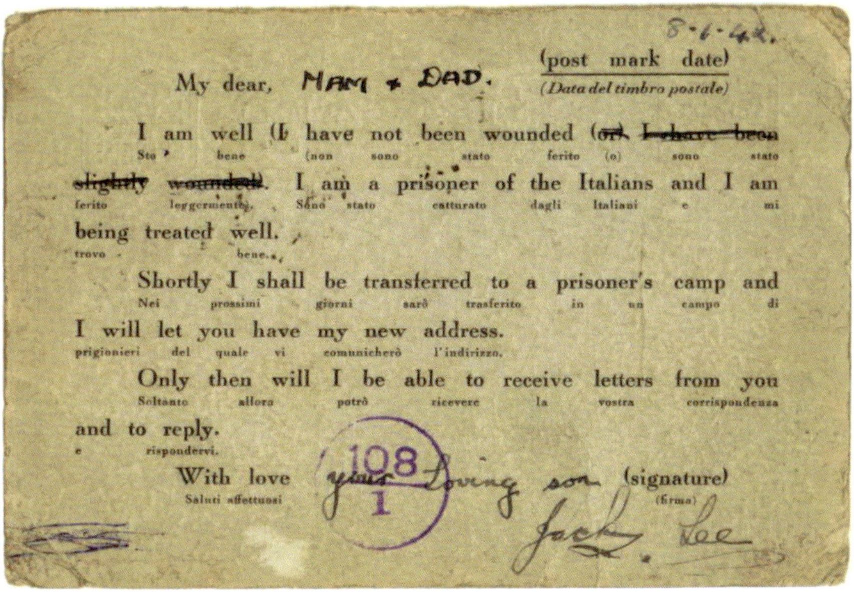
8-6-42.

My dear, MAM & DAD. (post mark date) (Data del timbro postale)

I am well (I have not been wounded (~~or) I have been slightly wounded~~). I am a prisoner of the Italians and I am being treated well.
Sto bene (non sono stato ferito (o) sono stato ferito leggermente). Sono stato catturato dagli Italiani e mi trovo bene.

Shortly I shall be transferred to a prisoner's camp and I will let you have my new address.
Nei prossimi giorni sarò trasferito in un campo di prigionieri del quale vi comunicherò l'indirizzo.

Only then will I be able to receive letters from you and to reply.
Soltanto allora potrò ricevere la vostra corrispondenza e rispondervi.

With love ~~your~~ loving son (signature)
Saluti affettuosi (firma)

Jack Lee

108
1

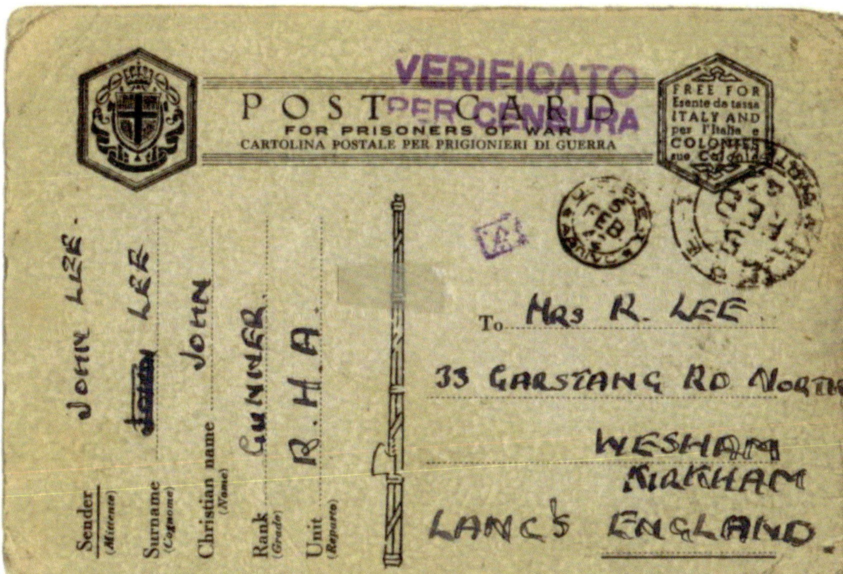
VERIFICATO PER CENSURA

POST CARD
FOR PRISONERS OF WAR
CARTOLINA POSTALE PER PRIGIONIERI DI GUERRA

FREE FOR
Esente da tassa
ITALY AND
per l'Italia e
COLONIES
sue Colonie

To Mrs R. LEE
33 GARSTANG RD NORTH
WESHAM
KIRKHAM
LANCS ENGLAND

Sender (Mittente) JOHN LEE.
Surname (Cognome) ~~JOHN~~ LEE
Christian name (Nome) JOHN
Rank (Grado) GUNNER
Unit (Reparto) R.H.A.

1942
Letter home to Mam and Dad

keen and we enjoyed the sport.

The bugle call was obvious on Sunday mornings too, during denominational church services, but not while the Catholic Mass was taking place. Representatives from the Vatican visited all the internment camps throughout Italy, to mingle and chat with army personnel. They asked how they could best help us and were instrumental in notifying our parents that we were safe and well through Vatican Radio. Written confirmation followed later from the Red Cross.

A lady in England heard my name and address mentioned on her radio and immediately wrote to my mother to give her the news. It was the first positive information my family had received since the letter from the War Office, notifying them that I had been posted missing in action. After the Vatican representative's visit, they provided all football strips, including socks and boots for our international matches. They also supplied musical instruments for an entertainment band, because many internees professed musical talents.

It never ceased to amaze me, how inventive some people were. One of our lads, a London-based motor mechanic in civvy street, devised a simple can-opener. He used half a worn metal heel from an army boot, a split wooden twig bound with string for the handle, and a bent nail extracted from his bed frame to make a lever.

For us, this was a remarkable achievement, since previously we had used either scissors or knives with difficulty. Even those tools would have been confiscated had they been found. Sharp instruments were definitely not allowed.

At regular intervals, the Italian patrols held random checks throughout the barracks, to see if we were using or making anything suspicious looking, or anything with a bit of imagination which they thought might be used in an escape attempt. As soon as a search patrol was apparent, the person nearest the door would shout, “Red Light,” the recognised code for us to hide everything.

Our barrack room was numbered fourteen. It was next door to an unoccupied one, where church services and recreational activities were held. Number sixteen was adjacent to the perimeter wall, a distance of approximately fourteen feet. Outside the wall was the guards’ barrack room, built on a raised platform eighteen inches high. One of the prisoners from hut sixteen, a mechanical engineer by trade, masterminded an escape plot. His men took down eight foot lengths of the main wooden timbers from the roof trusses. They supported a tunnel from beneath one of their bunks, under the wall and the guards' barracks to an exit beyond.

The men worked in gangs bringing out earth in their 'pillows' sandbags and scattering it under their hut, which was built on a two-foot high brick foundation. Taking turns to watch and listen for many hours to guard activities and conversations, they discovered every last detail of their movements and timetables.

The day before their planned escape, armed Italian guards entered hut sixteen, removed the bunks and exposed the excavation. Luckily, no-one was found in the tunnel. All men denied knowledge of it so there were no immediate reprisals.

A suspected 'foreign' informer was transferred to another camp. All the internees knew who it was and had he not been moved, I'm certain he would have been lynched.

The following week, new procedures were activated by the guards concerning all barracks with wooden floors. When they entered ours, the guards ordered us all to take our bunks outside. They then loosened part of the floor to obtain easy access at any given time. Every inch of soil on the foundation earth was finely raked. We were then allowed back inside with our bunks.

From that point onwards, often at 2.00am, the guards would

enter the barrack room with powerful searchlights to check that the earth under the floor boards remained undisturbed. Outside in the compound the earth around the huts was pierced at regular intervals with six-foot long, pointed metal stakes.

This made it impossible to plan any further tunnelling from our side of the road. The barracks on the opposite side however, had flag floors. How the prisoners in the end hut managed to support their escape route, I never knew, but the entrance was under a flag, again beneath a bunk. At the end of each evening's tunnelling activities, earth-filled sandbags were stacked directly underneath the entrance flag. This was because the guards periodically checked for tunnels by tapping the flags with pick axe handles to listen for hollow sounds.

Each time the flag was re-placed, the grotty, issued, putty-type soap was used as a filler to seal the crevices. After a dusting with fine soil the flag looked exactly like all the others. The tunnel was from the gable end of the barrack room, under a small disused plot of land, the trench and the wall, to surface under the building which housed the Red Cross parcels.

The men took turns for several days to watch Italian manoeuvres until they were satisfied they were adequately informed, then the escape date was set. It was to be on a Wednesday, the night before the laundry was exchanged, because there was always a roll call late on Thursday afternoons. It gave a full night and almost a day to clear the area.

Sixteen men escaped with a few provisions, mainly chocolate since it had been saved by numerous comrades and was easy to carry.

The seventeenth man, a chief submarine petty officer, tall and heavily built, was almost suffocated when the tunnel collapsed on him. Disaster at this stage was averted because he was immediately pulled clear by his friends and taken to the British Medical hut nearby. Two English doctors resuscitated him and covered for his feigned illness, hospitalising him for a few days.

When the sixteen escapees were eventually rounded up and recaptured, the seventeenth man was not recognised as one of their group. He was not only lucky to have survived the ordeal, but also to avoid the punishment, which was detention in the prison compound.

The prisoners were automatically searched as they were caught in their small groups and escorted back to camp. Because the main source of sustenance was discovered to be chocolate, as a reprisal from that incident onwards all chocolate bars and tinned goods in the Red Cross parcels were savagely attacked with claw hammers. Thus the 'life' of the food was limited, useless to store in the Mediterranean climate and useless to barter.

After the discovery of any escape attempt, all Red Cross parcels were cancelled for a few weeks - a bitter blow, making life more intolerable. We owe a debt of gratitude to the suppliers of the contents and to the Red Cross Organisation for delivering the parcels. These undoubtedly provided the 'highlights' and means of our survival during internment.

I was thrilled when I received my second parcel from home but I was furious that I wasn't allowed to keep the shoes and sandshoes in my parcel. My mother had saved her valuable coupons to acquire them from the Co-op. I complained to our Sergeant in charge who reported to R S M Peebles. The outcome was the Italian authorities said the goods had been confiscated in case I attempted to escape, but I could have them when I left the camp. My complaint was futile, I never saw the shoes or sandshoes again, not even when I left Servigliano.

I received my shirts, underclothes, and socks in parcels from home, they were very precious to me, many of the men unfortunately didn't receive home parcels and so had insufficient clothing. When their socks disintegrated they were issued with unbleached squares of cotton fabric as a poor alternative.

Time dragged dreadfully. During the summer months, it was scorching hot and we resorted to wearing only underpants and remaining in the shade as much as possible. The nights were cooler and tolerable. The winter weather was similar to our English climate. We experienced severe thunder and lightning storms at various intervals accompanied by torrential rain.

I wrote the allocated number of letters home on the regulation issue forms. My letters back were more like jigsaw puzzles. So much was censored, they were virtually useless news-wise, some items were even cut out. However I was reasonably contented in the knowledge that all was safe and well on the home front and that my family missed me equally as much as I missed them and dear old Blighty.

Since we had very little to do and all day in which to do it, a variety of boredom relieving occupations emerged. Apart from the recycling of tin cans previously mentioned, cooking, wood whittling and football, one sergeant in our unit collected old army socks from the entire camp. With the good unravelled wool from them, he knitted twelve-inch squares, to join and make a heavy winter blanket for himself.

An artistically talented soldier from one of the tank regiments, engraved a beautiful tank on his dixie with a pair of scissors. It was an enviable masterpiece and shone like silver when polished, using only earth, a rag soaked in water, elbow grease and a tremendous amount of patience.

As an alternative to football the Italians erected a boxing ring, and asked for volunteers. An incentive of their dingy double rations was insufficient enticement. There were no takers. We were all of the same opinion, we decided we weren't going to knock hell out of each other for the sake of a ladle of macaroni. That form of entertainment was a non-starter.

Card schools were held, not for gambling, simply to pass the time. It was an evening alternative to general chat and joke-telling in an attempt to keep up morale.

Towards the end of May 1943, our camp leader informed our unit that thirty men were to be sent to a working camp farm in Vigevano in Northern Italy. It appeared to be by random selection and I found myself included in this number. I had a good large canvas bag, which my mother had made and sent to me. This I used to carry all my possessions a few days later, when we departed Servigliano by train to arrive at Vigevano on June 3rd.

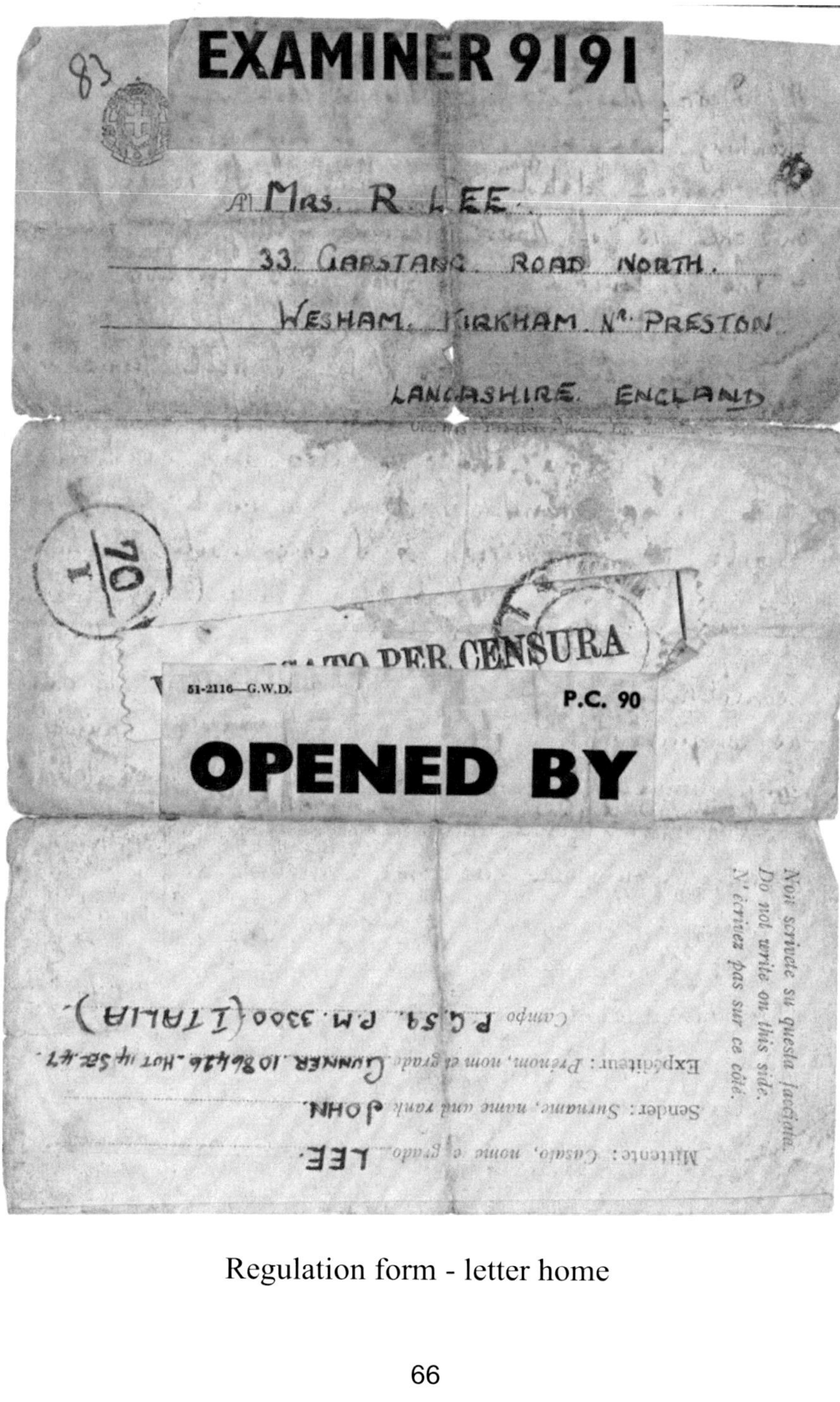
EXAMINER 9191

Al Mrs. R. LEE.

33. Garstang Road North.

Wesham. Kirkham. Nr. Preston

Lancashire. England

P.C. 90

OPENED BY

Non scrivete su questa facciata.
Do not write on this side.
N'écrivez pas sur ce côté.

Mittente: Casato, nome e grado LEE.
Sender: Surname, name and rank JOHN.
Expéditeur: Prénom, nom et grade Gunner.
Campo P.G. 59. P.M. 3300 (ITALIA).

Regulation form - letter home

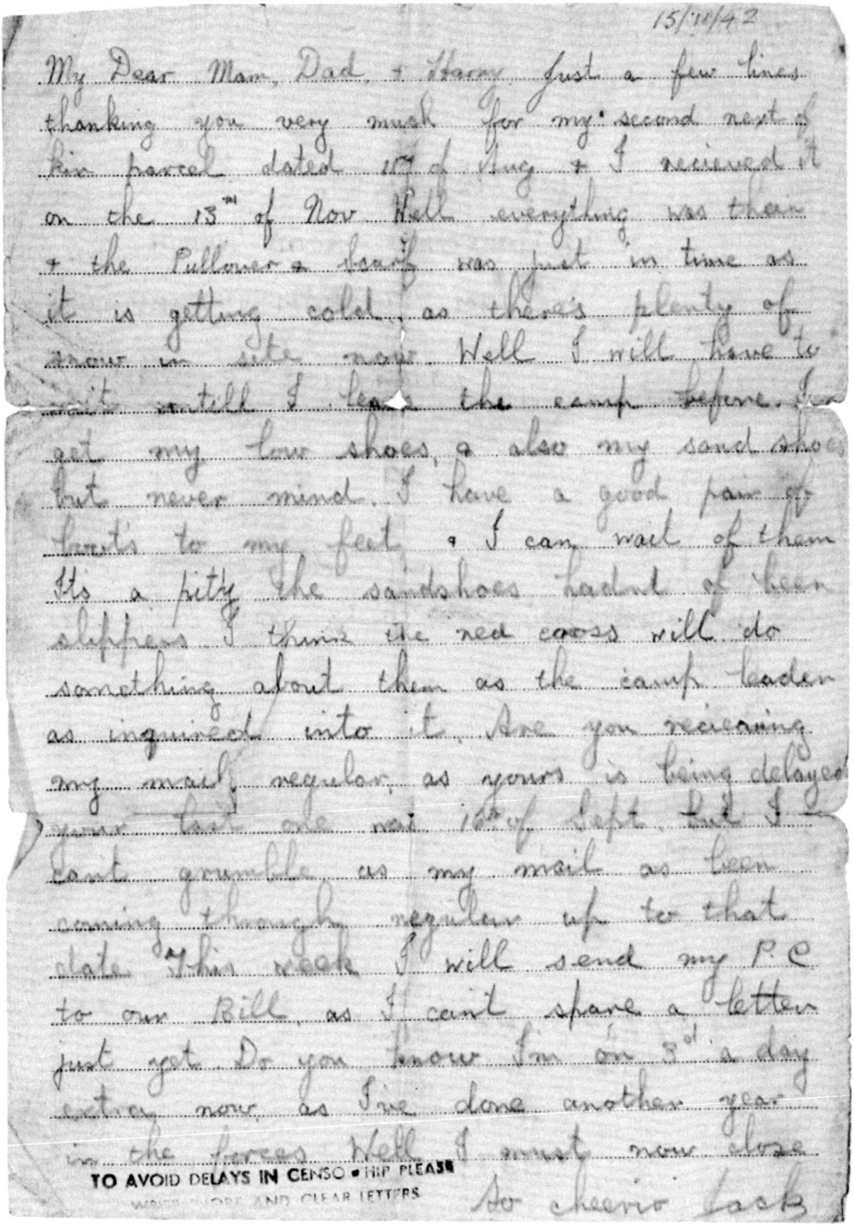
15/11/42

My Dear Mam, Dad + Harry just a few lines
thanking you very much for my second next of
kin parcel dated 17 of Aug + I recieved it
on the 13th of Nov Well everything was there
+ the Pullover + scarf was just in time as
it is getting cold as there's plenty of
snow in site now. Well I will have to
wait untill I leave the camp before I
get my low shoes + also my sand shoes
but never mind I have a good pair of
boots to my feet + I can wait of them
It's a pity the sandshoes hadnt of been
slippers I think the red cross will do
something about them as the camp leader
as inquired into it. Are you recieving
my mail regular, as yours is being delayed
your last one was 16th of Sept but I
cant grumble as my mail as been
coming through regular up to that
date This week I will send my P.C
to our Bill as I cant spare a letter
just yet. Do you know I'm on 3d a day
extra now as I've done another year
in the forces Well I must now close

TO AVOID DELAYS IN CENSO HIP PLEASE
WRI ORT AND CLEAR LETTERS

So cheerio Jack

The letter home

CHAPTER EIGHT
THE WORKING PARTY – VIGEVANO & CAPITULATION

At Vigevano we were billeted in a converted granary belonging to a local farmer. We had no contact with him, it was simply a base. We were split into three units to work at separate established family farms. Regrettably for the Italians, most of their able-bodied village men had also been conscripted, so we supplied the demand for labourers.

The granary contained double bunks, with a toilet and washing facilities at one end. It was built in the corner of a forty-foot yard, adjacent to a stream and surrounded by a retaining fence eight-foot high. There was a convenient alcove in the corner of the fence to allow the stream to flow through, where we were able to paddle and wash our clothes.

We soon discovered the main disadvantage at Vigevano was our rat-infested accommodation. Each night the numerous creatures scampered along the roof trusses covering all below with dust and debris. It was difficult to sleep because of the continuous scratching as the rodents scuttled about. Our shower unit in the corner consisted of a three-quarter-inch conduit pipe from the ceiling attached to a copper rose. Nimbly, the cheeky rats used acrobatic skills to climb down the pipe and drink the water while we showered.

We were also plagued by swarms of mosquitoes inside the lofty building. At night it was so bad that one evening after tea we took all our bedding and belongings outside, then set fire to a bale of straw in the granary in an attempt to fumigate the nasty gnats. The results were only temporarily successful. Because of the abundant water supply and in the conducive temperature, it wasn't long before the next cycle of mosquitoes was ready to invade. Whilst working outside we were constantly attacked by vicious horseflies. Their main objective appeared to be syphoning blood; causing infections, scabs and discomfort. One member of our group was so severely infected, he had to be confined in hospital, where he was captured by the Germans when Italy capitulated.

There were twelve men in our working party and we were escorted by an armed guard every weekday to a neighbouring farm about two miles away. Our first assignment was to assist with the potato harvest, handpicking and bagging them after they had been unearthed by a primitive rusty machine drawn by two oxen. The tedium of the operation was minimised because we worked alongside beautiful young Italian women, probably equivalent to our British Land Army girls. In spite of the language barrier we had many good laughs and sing-a-longs.

One of the women, whose husband was a prisoner of war in England, constantly sought reassurance that he would be well-treated by his British captors. We were able to console her and were positive he was in safer hands, living under much better circumstances then we had been.

At the end of each day, we took off our shirts and knotted the sleeves to make bags to carry as many of the potatoes as we could back to our quarters. We also acquired large beef tomatoes plucked fresh from outdoor plants and carried them in the same manner. The farmers didn't appear to mind; we didn't stop to ask.

It only took four days, twelve men and twelve women to complete the potato harvest, after which we laboured at the base farm for a few days. The maize had been cut and stacked to dry. It was then forked into a hay cart and taken for threshing. One of our lads was absolutely useless with a hay fork, displaying neither initiative nor aptitude. With the fork prongs the wrong way round he managed to spear the foot of the Italian loading on top of the cart. They always worked barefooted.

Following this chore, we turned cut wheat very primitively with long sharp sticks. It dried very quickly in the hot Mediterranean climate. It was at Vigevano I celebrated my twenty-third birthday, in solitary spirit only, I didn't tell anyone.

Apart from the rats and the flies, working conditions were better than last year and we weren't going to starve, because as far as food was concerned we fared very well. The freshly picked vegetables, potatoes, tomatoes and butter beans added to the cooking pot of macaroni supplementing our Red Cross supplies.

On the 6th July we received our first Italian issue of twenty five cigarettes plus a packet of tobacco.

Another parcel from home arrived on July 8th via Servigliano. It contained mainly clothes, socks, a cardigan, a jumper, a scarf, a tin of Rothmans cigarettes and some chocolate. I was extremely grateful for these presents, knowing the situation at home and how my parents must have scrimped and deprived themselves, because even clothing was rationed.

When we resumed work at our original farm, we were given hand sickles and ordered to cut the overgrown grass along both sides of a steep dyke embankment. It looked easily eight foot deep.

My brain froze momentarily. I have an intense aversion to frogs and other slimy creatures which I thought may have been lurking in the unknown depths of the murky water. Nothing, nothing was going to get me down there.

When I was ordered to begin, I said,

"No! I'm not going down there!"

The rifle was pointing at me. At first I thought the guard was going to shoot, but he was just astonished and demanded to know,

"Why not?"

I was already very hot, but I felt the perspiration and colour rise to my face as all eyes were directed disbelievingly towards me. Feverishly my brain raced to reach a realistic reason, then awkwardly I blurted out, “I'm bothered with rheumatics.”

The guard and the farmer had a heated conversation with lots of hand signals, consequently, I was marched back to our quarters and confined there for a whole week. The other members of my working party, amazed at my audacity, proceeded to clear the dyke with no further objections.

I wasn't unduly concerned, I had a week off work, but coincidentally the situation was diffused because a request for a joiner came through from the Italian officer in charge. Even though I had no training, I'd previously rewritten my occupation as a joiner on my identification forms, so I volunteered. The problem of deciding my fate had been resolved, I was accepted as a fully-fledged joiner.

I was lucky, I worked alone in my new career and with the few primitive tools at my disposal, I had the time and opportunity to experiment as I went along. I was asked to make seed potato trays from much larger boxes, that was easy. I was responsible for general maintenance work, like repairing farm carts and equipment. I even carved wooden sandal soles for the Italian guards as their footwear was extremely dilapidated. They asked if they could have our old socks, even though they were virtually useless when we had finished with them.

While I was involved in joinery tasks the other lads were picking rice in paddy fields. It was loaded onto carts on large wooden rollers and pulled by oxen.

The Italian women helped too. They wore aprons with large pockets in which they collected frogs. A rare delicacy for them and a valuable protein source, but I was relieved I wasn't involved.

When the day's manual wheat threshing for the men had finished, they were very dirty with dry dust and perspiration. They were allowed a refreshing swim in the river at the lower end of the farm where a bridge spanned the river.

On one hot day, ten men approached the river from the bank, but the eleventh, a London postman and an expert swimmer, decided to dive from the bridge. Although the water ran deep, he hit his head on a rock and broke his neck.

It was a traumatic experience. The guard was hysterical shouting and screaming. He was responsible for our welfare and would no doubt be severely reprimanded. Italian civilians tried desperately to revive the swimmer but to no avail. He was carried on a mule-drawn cart to the village mortuary.

One of our lads, a master tailor from Ulverston, acquired a white sheet and pieces of royal blue and scarlet material from the local women. He deftly created a brilliant Union Jack flag. It ceremoniously covered the simple wooden coffin in which the corpse was placed in full battledress.

The day of the funeral was painfully long and emotional for us all. The Italians mourned with us. He had been respected as a good comrade, it was like losing a brother. Even though it was a pure accident we all felt it should never have happened. After the service and burial in the Catholic cemetery, the parishioners took it upon themselves to maintain the grave, while for us all, further swimming was forbidden.

We were kept pretty much in the dark regarding Hitler's conquests in other parts of the world. Propaganda, morale-boosting messages for his allies, did nothing to alleviate our anxieties. However, early in September 1943, there was cause for a sudden dramatic turning point in our immediate situation.

From local radio, it transpired that Mussolini was firmly

convinced the end of the war was imminent and surrendered. When this occurred, the jubilant news reached us as we worked at Vigevano. We downed tools excitedly, as the farmer's son asked us to report to the farm house. This was most unusual since previously we had been denied access.

The Italians were ecstatic and greeted us as equals. An enormous buffet spread was laid out for everybody on the huge farm table. We were wined and dined as honoured guests.

Our last two mile journey back to base wasn't the usual route march, there was no armed guard. The news and the wine had achieved a wonderful sense of euphoria. We laughed and joked as we pranced along, singing all the old firm favourites like Roll out the Barrel, Tipperary and White Cliffs of Dover. The same spirit of elation greeted us as the other two working parties returned.

Most of us were outside chatting excitedly when the Camp Commandant entered the yard. Those men inside were ordered out to hear what he had to report. He said basically, that he no longer had any authority over us and since we were on Italian soil we were outside the jurisdiction of Germany – unless we were recaptured. As far as he was concerned, we were free to go if we wished. Tongue in cheek, he advised us to stay where we were, until he received further orders.

We held an impromptu meeting and were of the unanimous opinion that if we stayed put, the Germans would soon be along to pick us up. The villagers heard on their radios that Italians who helped prisoners would be shot. We therefore decided to leave as soon as possible. We formed groups, and twelve of us immediately prepared for the first leg of our homeward journey, we had a long way to go.

Once again my mother's canvas bag came in handy. Packing as many possessions and Red Cross food as it would comfortably hold, we took turns to carry it and made our way eastwards.

When we vacated Vigevano the villagers chopped down a section of the perimeter fence, to lead the Germans to believe we had escaped unaided.

CHAPTER NINE
ESCAPE TO SWITZERLAND

Keeping well clear of the main road for obvious reasons, we trekked through fields for a few miles until we reached a disused brick building. Sleeping on straw, head to toe we spent our first night of freedom there.

I awoke very early the following morning in agony. I had been bitten by a mosquito, or so our medical orderly thought. The right side of my face was painfully swollen and I could barely open my eyes. We had no antidote or medication to treat the infection. I was given two alternatives, either carry on and hope it would improve or return to Vigevano where the medical chest remained and collect a bottle of lotion.

Instinctively, I felt compelled to go back to Vigevano. I journeyed along, as quickly as possible, retracing our steps and remaining undercover.

Luckily the base was deserted. I found the bottle our Medical Officer had described and returned to find the group ready packed, awaiting my arrival and anxious to be on the hoof again, but northwards this time.

Once the treatment for my bite began, the pain and swelling on my face gradually eased, but it was a few days before I was back to normal.

An Italian partisan member contacted us. Even though he couldn't speak English, we could understand his hand signals. He got the message across that we had to move quickly. He didn't give us his name for security reasons, but he was so confident we trusted him implicitly. Because he was so familiar with the area he indicated that he would guide us to where we wouldn't be found.

For miles through the countryside he led us, well away from any roads, walking until dusk. We rested only for a few moments on a couple of occasions to take a few meagre bites of food. Exhausted, we camped by the River Ticino and slept the night on rocks in the seclusion of large bushes there.

Our guide returned to his home but was back the following morning on his bike, carrying a machete. He took us further up river to an even more secluded area where he immediately began to attack the smaller trees to build a hut. Like a demon he moved, proving the machete was no toy, indeed, he was a formidable force to be reckoned with.

As the residence neared completion, it was waterproofed and camouflaged with reeds and branches collected from the embankments. We were easily accommodated within, six men to each side, in what was to be our home for the following three weeks.

Our guide became an invaluable lifeline to us. He brought us fresh food supplies daily and, equally importantly, news about the war throughout Europe via the underground movement, which was more reliable than press propaganda.

Towards the end of the third week, he arrived in an agitated state, indicating that we must move on quickly. German soldiers were systematically searching all local cantons and would very soon be in our district.

Unknown to us, he had a small rowing boat concealed in undergrowth nearby and proceeded in his usual efficient manner to ferry us across the river, four at a time. When the last group was safely over, he returned alone to destroy all evidence of habitation. We watched the blaze as he fired the hut, it went up like a tinderbox until only charred embers remained.

We were concealed on a sandy knoll, surrounded and screened by trees. Our guide, having completed his tasks across the river, returned and the devilish dervishes with the machete began again. It was fascinating to watch how speedily he made a small clearing. Selecting two tall trees about twelve feet apart, he directed us to construct a framework to support a large white canvas sheet which made a tent. From nearby trees he cut many leafy branches for camouflage.

He signed to us that German spotter planes often flew down river and that as the foliage withered, it would need to be replaced with fresh branches. Before he left on his bike he indicated that if we remained quiet, no-one would know of our existence.

The following day he brought twelve, ten-inch, heavy duty, white dinner plates with fresh food. We squatted cross-legged on the sandy floor of the clearing to eat.

One day, just after the plates had been laid out ready for lunch, we heard the unmistakable drone of a distant engine becoming louder as it approached. We flung our bodies over the plates on the ground and remained motionless until the aeroplane had flown over.

It was a tense few moments for us, we were relieved we hadn't been spotted. No doubt the circular formation of the plates would have beckoned like a beacon had they not been covered.

Apart from the domestic chores, washing, cooking and replacing tent camouflage, there was little we could do. Although we were confined and totally dependent on our guide, we were reasonably happy in our new-found freedom as we bathed in the warm river and soaked up the October sunshine.

Early one morning, during the fifth week of our encampment, we were alarmed to hear the obvious sounds of something or someone approaching.

I could only think the worst, that our number was up. We had no guns or weapons to resist attack. The suspense was agonising as we waited apprehensively to meet our foe face to face.

He was alone, an armed uniformed officer, well-built and easily six-foot tall. I couldn't decide whether he belonged to the German or Italian army until he spoke and it was neither. He was merely an Italian gamekeeper named Tenente Pino, patrolling his territory. We gave him the fright of his life, we weren't the sort of game he had expected to encounter.

Providence appeared to have intervened on our behalf, he asked what we needed and became our loyal friend. Although his family hadn't much to offer, he supplied us with food and cigarettes. On subsequent visits he brought along his teenage daughter to help carry the provisions.

We remained in seclusion for a further two months, but our evacuation was necessitated by the rising level of the river when the rains came.

We were advised to be ready to move within the next couple of days, it was anticipated the clearing would then be under water.

One of the lads with ash-blonde hair was told to black it with boot polish supplied by our guide. He looked like an Italian when we left, the disguise worked. Later, during rainy conditions on the Alps, he looked awful when streaky, black dye poured down his face, but by then the danger was over. Milan was to be our next critical destination.

Our guide provided civilian clothes to make us less conspicuous. I had a brown, checked jacket, a navy-blue trilby, blue trousers, and low, brown shoes. Tenente said, it was advisable to take only one small parcel, minimal toiletries, anything more would arouse suspicion.

Articles of clothing we didn't require were shared between our guide and the gamekeeper and were sadly carried off in my exclusive canvas bag.

Fortunately our tracks were covered, but the invaluable tent sheeting was recovered before the area was left to the elements to complete the job.

After leaving the seclusion of the wooded area by the river, in the early hours of the morning on 2nd December, we walked to Abbiategrasso railway station. Tickets had been acquired in advance for us. We arrived in darkness at 7.30am, in time to catch a goods train to take us to the outskirts of Milan. From there, following instructions we boarded a train for a forty minute journey to the city centre.

Accompanied by our guide, we were briefed to walk along the pavement at a discreet distance of about ten yards behind each other. We were to observe the colleague in front and follow his actions.

The chap I followed stopped outside a large, disused, double-fronted shop in a side street. After a pre-arranged number of knocks, the door shutter was raised and he was admitted. The same procedure was carried out at regular intervals until we were all safely inside.

We were immensely relieved to be ushered into a larger store room at the rear, where we were welcomed with food, drinks and cigarettes. We had entered the temporary safety of a cell of one of the underground resistance movement collecting points. The atmosphere was electric. The entire building was practically bulging with service men, all British Nationals, also en route to freedom.

The Italian partisan who had guided us since leaving Vigevano, bade us bon voyage and returned to continue with his own clandestine war efforts while we acquired a new guide. He informed us we would be leaving later the same day.

Plans were aborted. A vital message filtered through, another partisan member arrived to tell us distressfully through an interpreter that the previous day's party of escapees had been captured by the Germans. His contact couldn't give precise details, it could have been at any point between Caslino and the Alps - the neutral Swiss border.

We were advised it would be unsafe to leave within the next twenty-four hours. We were to await further confirmation that all was clear before attempting to continue our journey.

Regardless of the severity of the situation, our spirits remained apprehensively high. We appreciated an evening meal and spent the night comfortably confident in the company of our courageous hosts. During the afternoon of the following day, the message we eagerly anticipated arrived and we were able to resume our journey.

Following a similar exit pattern, only in reverse to the one to gain entry, we left the shop one at a time, heading for Milan railway station. We had been briefed by our new guide to try to appear casual and relaxed.

There were numerous large glass-fronted shops on three sides of the station. We were to gaze discreetly into the windows, whilst keeping the colleague in front under observation. When we boarded the train we were advised to avoid conversation with other passengers at all costs, to pretend to sleep or read a newspaper. Our guide told us the journey to Caslino would take approximately two hours. His signal to us, to prepare to alight at the following stop, would be when he walked the length of the train whistling Lili Marlene. If any members of our party got lost or missed the train, the pick-up procedure was to report to the nearest church, where we would be hidden until it was convenient for us to be collected and returned to the cell base. All eventualities were covered. We were at last thankfully happy to receive a small portion of food to sustain us and be on our way.

There was a heavy German presence outside Milan railway station. Soldiers mingled amongst the crowded thoroughfare as teatime commuters assembled. Again, our tickets were obtained in advance, we passed through the barriers without incident and made a bee-line for the shop windows, trying desperately to appear calm and casual. My heart was beating fifty to the dozen. It was December and I was perspiring profusely. After what appeared to be only a minute or so, I looked round to check my colleague's position. He wasn't there, neither could I see any of our men. I thought my head would burst with the throbbing palpitations in my temples, and that at any moment someone would notice my agitation. I had no idea which direction my colleagues had taken.

Further down one of the tracks a linesman was busily working. With the little Italian I had picked up, I asked,

"Which train is going to Caslino?"

He looked up at me like a startled rabbit, his eyeballs protruding in shock. It unnerved me so much I thought I'd blown my chance to escape.

Convinced I was under suspicion, without waiting for a reply, I ran until I saw a list of place names chalked on a blackboard at the buffers. Recognising the name Caslino halfway down, I jumped aboard the grimy train standing there.

I worked my way through many compartments until with a sigh of relief I eventually recognised one of our men.

The train was packed to capacity, this I hadn't bargained for. There were no seats available and very little standing room in the corridors. I found a spare strap to hang on to and hoped no one would notice my legs wobbling like jelly.

As the train pulled out, the tension gradually eased. Completely relaxed now, I allowed myself to swing naturally with the rhythmical momentum as we gathered speed. I strained my neck but could see very little through the dusty grey, opaque windows. After several stops and what appeared an eternity, I heard the distant strains of the pre-arranged signal.

"Underneath the lamplight..."

Our whistling guide, pushed his way zealously past walls of bodies in the compartment. Caslino was to be our next stop.

❧ ☙

We left the train as nonchalantly as possible following the leader through the exit and were led towards the lower contours of the Alps.

I was amazed when another party of eighteen men joined us, making our numbers up to thirty-one including the new guide. He was an Italian, in his fifties at a guess, a slightly built, wiry sort of fellow with a rugged, weather-beaten complexion. His hair and ears were completely concealed under a thick-knitted bob cap. He was dressed as a casual Italian labourer, appearing nimble-footed and very fit. He looked just the right type of person whose expertise and experience as a chaperone proved to be invaluable guiding charges over the country's roughest terrain.

❧ ☙

The gradual incline leading to the approach round the first summit began immediately. In single file we were led along a narrow track. I marvelled at the snowclad scenic views and occasional sightings of mountain goats, until deeper shades of dusk closed in around us. It was bitterly cold and icy underfoot. As we gained height, we were soon enveloped in low, moisture-laden clouds. The obscurity helped because we were unable to see the dangers below, but the freezing dampness collected in dewy droplets on our hair and clothes, wetting them through.

The ascent became more difficult until it was impossible to stand. Nature forced us to our hands and knees on the diminishing path. We clawed the vertical jagged rocks, frantically attempting to avoid the sheer drop on one side.

After an ordeal of several hours, we reached the becalmed shores of Lake Como. We were authorised to move as stealthily as possible because our route took us along a cobbled road and through an archway which formed dwellings with bedrooms above. The road led to a boathouse, from which our guide 'borrowed' a boat and rowed us across the lake six at a time.

We were on Italian territory, still under German jurisdiction if caught, until we reached the Swiss border, which was a further eight hours away.

The ascent round the second treacherous peak was even more dangerous than the first. It was sleeting, snowing, blowing, icy and extremely slippery. We were totally ill-clad for such an expedition.

The utility nature of our footwear soon became obvious. The synthetic soles parted company from the leather uppers and the compressed cardboard inner soles disintegrated completely under such harsh conditions.

My shoes weren't too bad, apart from letting in water, but the majority of the men were obliged to fasten their shoes on with handkerchiefs or whatever they were able to salvage as ties. As we climbed higher, the path narrowed to barely a ledge and we were forced to all fours again, clinging desperately for dear life. One slip and it would have been the end.

The altitude affected our breathing, our pace slowed down, we were constantly resting to breathe. We became so exhausted, doubts swamped our brains regarding our ability to continue. We were past chivvying each other along. We had very little energy left, our fingers and feet were numb with the icy coldness, and we were desperately hungry and dehydrated. We had only eaten the small portion of bread and meat the partisans gave us before leaving Milan the previous afternoon.

We resorted to eating snow and discovered we were unable to speak after taking only a small amount, nevertheless it quenched our thirst. We continued at snail's pace.

When dawn broke, we were still feverishly cold and wet, high in the clouds, trekking towards the border. I heard a whisper that our numbers were reduced, some members of our party had dropped out thoroughly fatigued.

I had to keep going, automatic reflexes and basic survival instincts appeared to drive me. The dawn only served to highlight the imminent dangers.

The doubts were back again, I didn't know how much longer I could keep up. It was extremely difficult weaving around the jagged rocks. Would I be the next one to fall by the wayside? It was a long way down.

I had come this far, I couldn't give up, I began to draw inner strength from the knowledge that I was on my way to freedom and home. So much nearer but still so far away.

Even at this stage I was conscious that the Germans could have us under observation as we pressed onwards. There was still the possibility that we could be picked up at any time or even shot.

Then came the realisation that we could breathe more easily, we were no longer climbing, the snow and ice was thawing to a squelch. The clouds gradually lifted and dispersed.

Although it remained very rocky underfoot, the path spread wider before us. I was conscious of water splish-splashing and tiny rivulets trickling down. We were descending.

I had no recollection of time, of how long we had been travelling or how far we had yet to go, but when in the distance we saw greenery, an overwhelming feeling that we must be nearly there became apparent amongst us.

Our pace quickened, so did our heartbeats, as with a sudden burst of energy and immense relief the objective of our mission came into focus. What remained of our bedraggled party approached the formidable wire fence, eight-foot high and guarded at only very infrequent intervals.

We were approached by a blue-uniformed, armed, soldier. I couldn't detect his nationality, but he blocked our path. One of the lads asked excitedly,

"Where is Switzerland?"

He understood but didn't speak and pointed to the earth beyond the fence. Thank goodness, he was a Swiss Guard. We were so relieved to have been brought safely to freedom.

After a brief conversation with our guide, the Swiss Guard helped us to climb the fence onto a sentry box on the Swiss side, thus reducing the drop for a softer landing.

We were asked to sign our names on some printed slips of paper our guide held. We did so willingly. I understood he received a fee from the British Government for each name. Even so, I regarded it a small price for the tremendous risk he had undertaken.

It's impossible to put a price on freedom and we were truly free, on neutral ground.

Regardless of our soggy state, the painful effects of the journey and the elements, the adrenalin flowed. Our spirits were sky high. We embraced our comrades, laughing and prancing about like spring lambs.

We waved our thankful farewells to the Alpine guide who returned to Caslino, while a new one appeared to lead us down to a community centre in the local village.

Such bliss, we deeply appreciated the delightfully welcoming meal, followed by the luxury of a hot shower, a change of clothing, and the first night of real freedom in a warm comfortable bed.

The Alps

The Alps

Switzerland

Unsuitable footwear

Switzerland

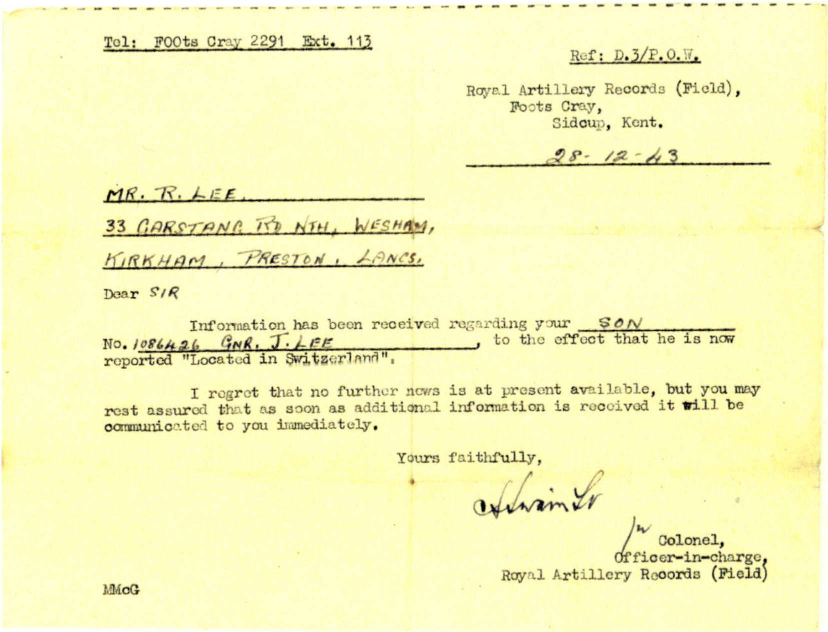

Tel: FOOts Cray 2291 Ext. 113

Ref: D.3/P.O.W.

Royal Artillery Records (Field),
Foots Cray,
Sidcup, Kent.

28-12-43

MR. R. LEE.
33 GARSTANG RD NTH, WESHAM,
KIRKHAM, PRESTON, LANCS.

Dear SIR

Information has been received regarding your SON No. 1086426 GNR. J. LEE, to the effect that he is now reported "Located in Switzerland".

I regret that no further news is at present available, but you may rest assured that as soon as additional information is received it will be communicated to you immediately.

Yours faithfully,

[signature]

/w Colonel,
Officer-in-charge,
Royal Artillery Records (Field)

MMcG

Letter saying Jack was reported located in Switzerland

Switzerland
New Kit

CHAPTER TEN
SWITZERLAND & HOMEWARD BOUND

It was December 5th 1943. My first day in Switzerland was like awakening from recurring nightmares.

The Swiss authorities took particulars from all escapees to inform next of kin, which my family duly received with immense relief.

We were unable to return to England because we were landlocked, the Germans occupied all the border territories.

After a thorough medical, I was kitted out with a new British Army battledress, a black beret, boots and a good-sized grey canvas ruck sack.

We were transported by rail to a small village called Elsau, at an estimate of about sixty miles away.

Our billet for the following three months was to be the local school. The dining room was upstairs and food was plentiful, especially when the Red Cross parcels began to arrive for us.

The local civilians were most helpful, the women washed and mended our clothes. This included knitting in the holes of our socks and a good job they made too, making the repairs almost invisible.

Many of the men took occupations locally wherever possible. Several were employed bark stripping in the lumbering industry.

I volunteered to assist in Elsau's footwear workshop, repairing army personnel boots and stitching by hand leather straps to strengthen rucksacks.

The only experience I'd previously had was watching the old village cobbler as a boy. Work in the slipper factory had been totally different, mainly with machinery. At Elsau I gained the expertise of a British master craftsman, Joe Simpkin, whose civvy street occupation was in the boot and shoe industry at Leicester.

I didn't earn much money, but it gave me a little more independence, enabling me to participate in some of the local customs and amenities, especially when it was my twenty-fourth birthday. This one I could really celebrate.

A gang of us spent the evening in the local pub sampling Schnapps straight from the barrel, which was very cheap. In appearance it resembled clear water and had such a pleasant taste, we drank it by the tumbler full, finding it extremely exhilarating.

When the fresh air hit me outside, POW, I was absolutely legless, but I wasn't the only one. We were an excessively inebriated squad and supported each other back to billet. I don't remember any details, but I was as right as rain the following morning. Some of my mates looked a bit groggy, but we had all enjoyed the occasion.

We played local teams at five-a-side football and exercised to strengthen muscles and redevelop skills after the Italian ordeal.

From Elsau we were taken on a superb scenic route by rail to Adelboden, a holiday resort in the mountains. I think it was to vacate our quarters to make room for other prisoners who were flooding in, taking advantage of the neutrality and hospitality of Switzerland.

A single-decker bus took us up the steep snowclad gradients to wooden chalets, where we were accommodated for a further three months.

Our sloping rooftop was ideal for sunbathing. At over two thousand feet above sea level the air was pure and invigorating, excellent convalescing conditions for chesty ailments.

I enjoyed some of the winter sporting activities, when the bowling green and tennis courts were converted into ice-rinks. I

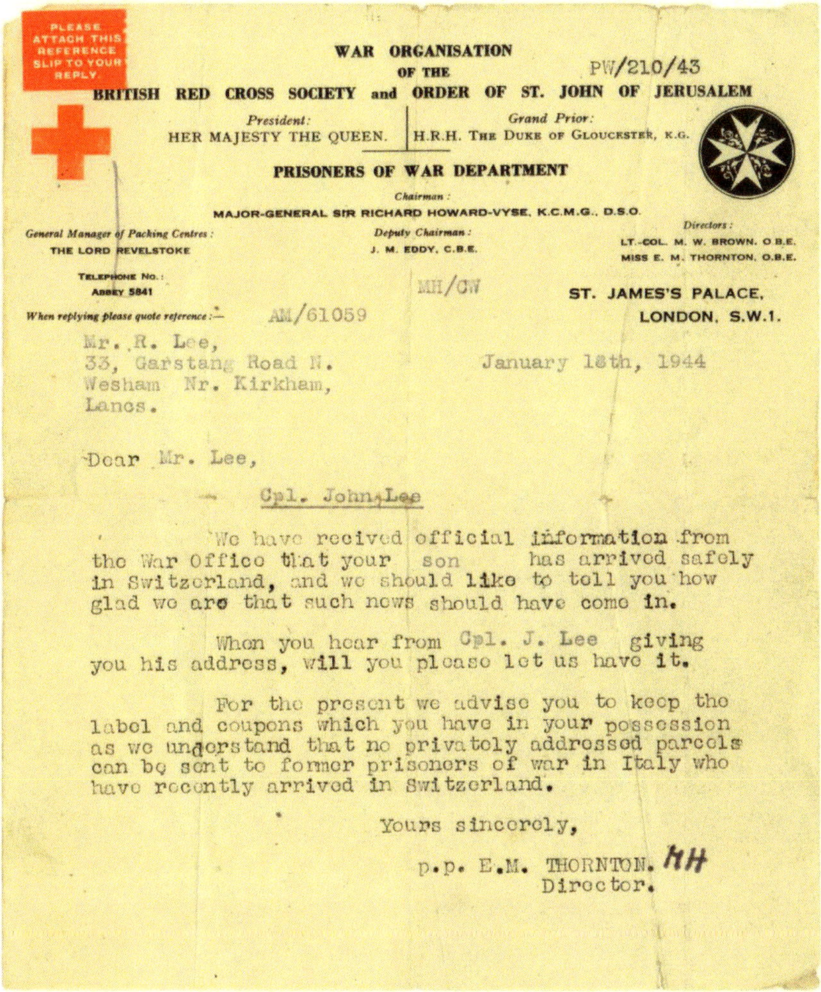

PLEASE ATTACH THIS REFERENCE SLIP TO YOUR REPLY.

PW/210/43

WAR ORGANISATION
OF THE
BRITISH RED CROSS SOCIETY and ORDER OF ST. JOHN OF JERUSALEM

President: HER MAJESTY THE QUEEN.
Grand Prior: H.R.H. THE DUKE OF GLOUCESTER, K.G.

PRISONERS OF WAR DEPARTMENT

Chairman:
MAJOR-GENERAL SIR RICHARD HOWARD-VYSE, K.C.M.G., D.S.O.

General Manager of Packing Centres: THE LORD REVELSTOKE
Deputy Chairman: J. M. EDDY, C.B.E.
Directors: LT.-COL. M. W. BROWN, O.B.E. MISS E. M. THORNTON, O.B.E.

TELEPHONE No.: ABBEY 5841

MH/CW

ST. JAMES'S PALACE,
LONDON, S.W.1.

When replying please quote reference:— AM/61059

Mr. R. Lee,
33, Garstang Road N.
Wesham Nr. Kirkham,
Lancs.

January 18th, 1944

Dear Mr. Lee,

Cpl. John Lee

We have recived official information from the War Office that your son has arrived safely in Switzerland, and we should like to tell you how glad we are that such news should have come in.

When you hear from Cpl. J. Lee giving you his address, will you please let us have it.

For the present we advise you to keep the label and coupons which you have in your possession as we understand that no privately addressed parcels can be sent to former prisoners of war in Italy who have recently arrived in Switzerland.

Yours sincerely,

p.p. E.M. THORNTON. MH
Director.

Arosa Red Cross letter home

Le porteur:

Gnr. J. Lee

Le commandant:

Lager für entwichene Kriegsgefangene

Arosa

Der Kommandant:

DÜTSCHLER OBLT.

COMMISSARIAT FÉDÉRAL
à l'Internement et à l'Hospitalisation

Carte d'Identité provisoire
pour militaire étranger.

№ 005312

Le porteur de la présente déclare se nommer:

LEE. J. 1086426

fils de RICHARD LEE né le 13-6-20.

à WESHAM (LANCS) province ENGLAND.

profession JOINER.

incorporation 1086426 ARMY.

Cette carte ne peut servir de document officiel; elle ne tient lieu que de carte d'identité personnelle.

Signature au verso!

Arosa new document

Happier times Arosa

learnt to skate, but wasn't keen on skiing. A few of our lads became so proficient they were awarded medals for winning competitions. Curling was another popular game with the locals which I enjoyed watching.

Once more we were moved to make way for others and to join a larger established group, which was situated near a main rail-link to France and appeared to be a collecting point for prisoners of all nationalities. It was to Arosa, our final destination in Switzerland, back to sea level, to stay in a luxurious holiday hotel, where we enjoyed the amenities at our disposal as well as the scenery and the summer sun.

Four of us found ourselves worthy occupations, providing NAAFI facilities, selling chocolates, cigarettes and hot drinks. One of my simple tasks was to ensure that the electric water heater was constantly full and boiling, ready to serve tea and coffee on demand to the lads. This continued right up to October and the money we earned bought numerous souvenirs to take home.

We departed Arosa by rail on October 4th 1944, our destination Marseilles via Genoa.

Some of the Partisans had advance knowledge of our journey and as we travelled through France, gave us their salute at two of the stations. They lined up on the platforms and presented arms as our troop train slowed down to pass through. It was totally unexpected and their noble gesture made me feel immensely proud.

At Marseilles, the American forces provided excellent hospitality for us whilst awaiting our departure from France, until the last evening, when we slept under canvas. After that final night on foreign soil we were transported to the harbour, where we boarded a flat-bottomed boat which took us out to our troopship anchored off shore to sail the same morning. We berthed at Algiers, where members of the Red Cross boarded to greet us, supplying chocolates and cigarettes.

On the 15th October we departed Algiers in convoy with twelve other vessels, our hopes sky high in anticipation of the final part of our journey to beloved 'Blighty'.

We were fortunate to avoid enemy observation during the voyage home but even so, all was not plain sailing. Crossing the Bay of Biscay in the North Atlantic Ocean, we experienced a turbulent time in exceedingly rough weather. The waves were whipped into a foaming frenzy several feet high. An empty tank transporting vessel immediately ahead of our carrier was bobbing about in all directions like a weightless cork. It was regarded as a source of imminent danger and ordered to the rear of the convoy.

Much later, in becalmed waters, I sensed the journey's end approaching. We sailed from the Atlantic into the Firth of Clyde and up the estuary, to the back drop of Scotland's picturesque majestic mountains.

We dropped anchor in the Clyde Basin on October 23rd 1944. Although we were obliged to spend another night on board, we were in good company. We slept alongside the Queen Elizabeth and the Queen Mary, almost unrecognisable in their wartime 'greys', and many other vessels moored for safety within the boom.

During breakfast the following morning, we were alerted by the unmistakable droning of our engines in the shallower waters of the river.

We charged from our tables, many of us taking our drinks of tea to the ships rails. Immediately, the voice of authority boomed through the tannoy.

"Attention all personnel! This is your captain speaking. Will you please even yourselves out, otherwise you will all have to go below deck! The ship is listing heavily towards starboard."

I was already next to the rail, but sensibly the lads did spread out until we maintained an even keel.

We berthed at King George V Docks to a tumultuous welcome, a sea of happy faces, waving flags, and a full military band greeted us playing 'Roll out the Barrel'. We accompanied the rhythm by banging our enamelled mugs on the metal rails and singing along.

Words couldn't describe my ecstatic feeling, but they were tinged with conflicting anguish for the families of comrades who would not be returning.

Before disembarking, one of the shore officers asked,

"What about customs and excise?"

Another officer with a broad Scottish accent replied,

"Customs! Customs! These lads are ex-prisoners of war. They have nothing to declare."

We didn't hang about. As soon as the gangplank was down, we were off, almost twelve-hundred of us, well and truly on British soil.

Our troop-train was nearby, ready to take us to a camp at Beaconsfield, ironically, we had heard it had been previously occupied by prisoners of war from Italy.

After my final medical and receiving the African Star ribbon, I was released with a travel warrant, six weeks' pay and double ration coupons for repatriation leave. Then without further incident, I was homeward bound to Wesham, near Preston, to the heart of Lancashire's green and beautiful Fylde, for a truly memorable family reunion.

Sixty Swiss Misses are brides of Britons

SOLDIER-INTERNEES HOME AGAIN

News Chronicle Reporter

OVER 1,100 Service men arrived at a North-West port yesterday after internment in Switzerland for periods ranging from months to years.

They were given an official welcome. After disembarkation the repatriates will travel south to a reception camp, and leave will follow.

As the ship docked, the men gave loud cheers and rattled tin mugs and plates on the rails of the ship. A military band greeted them with "Roll Out the Barrel."

Dressed in a variety of uniforms, including our own Army and Navy, they looked fit and cheerful and were soon exchanging jokes with dockers lined on the pierside.

All the men spoke highly of the Swiss people. About 60 have married Swiss girls.

Cpl. Gordon Poole, of Stockport, who was taken prisoner at Tobruk in 1942, told me that Switzerland was paradise after an Italian prisoner of war camp.

"Food is none too plentiful, even for the Swiss," he said, "but they gave us good as they had themselves. The Red Cross parcels were a great help and made life very comfortable for us.

"We lived in hotels, and had every freedom. Curfew hour was 10 p.m., but those who worked were allowed to stay out till 11. Other privileges were available when we were asked out as guests by Swiss families."

Gordon made his way into Switzerland after jumping a train in Italy which was taking him to Germany.

Lived in a wood

Commando Signaller Andrew Walker, of Glasgow, escaped while being taken from Italy to Germany.

He said the Italian people were very helpful, and besides giving him food and money sheltered him from the Germans on many occasions.

Private John Brown, of Barrhead, was captured at St. Valery in 1940, where he was serving with the original Highland Division, but he was a prisoner for only 16 days. He managed to escape when marching through Belgium to a prison camp in Germany.

"I lived for six months in a wood," said Brown, "then I made my way to Flanders, where I stayed with a farmer for over six months. After that I went to Brussels, where I spent a year being looked after by Belgian patriots.

"I had some narrow escapes from the Gestapo and things were becoming so hot that on Aug. 5, 1943, I got some maps together and inside a week I had reached Switzerland."

Sam Bridge, of Bury, said that he made his way to Milan after the Italian armistice. "The industrial workers were extremely anti-Fascist and were active in partisan groups," he said.

Back to "Blighty"

Pictures show below, the returned exiles crowd the deck rails to catch a first glimpse of "Blighty," and, above, with their mascot

Sixty Swiss Misses

Sixty Swiss Misses are brides of Britons SOLDIER - INTERNEES HOME AGAIN

Over 1,100 Service men arrived at a North West port yesterday after internment in Switzerland for periods ranging from months to years. They were given an official welcome. After disembarkation the repatriates will travel south to a reception camp and leave will follow.

As the ship docked, the men gave loud cheers and rattled tin mugs and plates on the rails of the ship. A military band greeted them with "Roll Out the Barrel." Dressed in a variety of uniforms, including our own Army and Navy, they looked fit and cheerful and were soon exchanging jokes with dockers lined on the pierside. All the men spoke highly of the Swiss people. About 60 have married Swiss girls.

Cpl. Gordon Poole, of Stockport, who was taken prisoner at Tobruk in 1942, told me that Switzerland was paradise after an Italian prisoner of war camp.

"Food was none too plentiful, even for the Swiss" he said "but they gave us good as they had themselves. The Red Cross parcels were a great help and made life very comfortable"

"We lived in hotels and had every freedom. Curfew hour was 10pm, but those who worked were allowed to stay till 11. Other privileges were available when we were asked out as guests of Swiss families" Gordon made his way into Switzerland after jumping a train in Italy which was taking him to Germany.

Lived in a wood

Commando Signaller Andrew Walker of Glasgow, escaped while being taken from Italy to Germany. He said the Italian people were very helpful, and besides giving him food and money, sheltered him from the Germans on many occasions.

Private John Brown, of Barrowhead, was captured at St. Valery in 1940, where he was serving with original Highland Division, but he was a prisoner for only 16 days. He managed to escape when marching through Belgium to a prison camp in Germany.

"I lived for 6 months in a wood" says Brown "then I made my way to Flanders, where I stayed with a farmer for over six months. After that I went to Brussels where I spent a year being looked after by Belgium patriots.

"I had some narrow escapes from the Gestapo and things were becoming so hot that on Aug 5th 1942, I got some maps together and inside a week I had reached Switzerland"

Sam Bridge of Bury, said that he made his way to Milan after the Italian armistice. "The industrial workers were extremely anti-fascit and were active in partisan groups" he said.

FUGITIVES FROM NAZIS HAD GRIM STRUGGLE TO REACH SWITZERLAND

Gnr. J. Lee

THE hardships endured by British prisoners of war, in escaping from enemy prison camps to Switzerland and have been vividly described to "Lancashire Daily Post" reporters, who have interviewed a number of men from this area.

Small Union Jacks, with the greeting "Welcome Home," fluttered over the rambler-covered porch of the old whitewashed cottage adjoining Brock Garage, Brock, near Garstang, the home of Gunner Thomas Holmes, 25-year-old son of Mr. and Mrs. Thomas Holmes, who has arrived home after internment in Switzerland, looking fit and well. He was one of the Service men who recently arrived at a North-West port.

Gunner Holmes, who was welcomed home by his father and mother, and members of the family, has had many thrilling experiences, which he unfolded to a "Lancashire Daily Post" reporter. He fought in Libya with the Eighth Army, being taken prisoner at Tobruk in June, 1942. From there he was sent to Tripoli, where, he says, the living conditions were then deplorable. There was a lot of casualties through lack of water, many dying of dysentery and starvation.

Food and water was so scarce that prisoners even sacrificed their private treasures, such as watches and rings, to get it.

Parcels from the Red Cross had not then got through.

Gunner Holmes was in concentration camps in Italy for 18 months before making his escape the day after the Italian capitulation.

"We crossed several rivers and made good our escape into Switzerland. We tramped over hundreds of miles, which took us two weeks, and had many narrow escapes from Fascists and German troops.

For two months in a prison camp, and another two months after my escape, I was barefoot, but on getting into Switzerland I managed to get a pair of boots, but they were much too small for me.

"My feet were swollen and tender with being without boots so long, and it was not long before I was minus four toe nails, and had two sore heels and a septic ankle. I crawled over the Alps on my hands and knees, as my feet were so sore. After being interrogated on the border, my pal and I were interned, and treated very well indeed. I worked in the gardens at an hotel for a time, and also did a spot of wood chopping."

RED CROSS PRAISED

Gunner Holmes, who joined the Army in March, 1940, was previously employed by his brother, Mr. W. H. Holmes, as a driver in his cattle removing business. He cannot speak too highly of the work of the Red Cross, and thanks many local people for their kindness to himself and his parents during the time he was a prisoner and interned. He was reported missing after his capture at Tobruk, and it was six months before his parents heard of his safety through a radio message from the Vatican City.

A brother, [illegible] James Holmes, is in Holland, and his youngest brother, Private Stanley Holmes, is also home on leave.

"A Closed Book"

Gunner Thos. Oddie, R.A., who has just arrived at his home in Coldstream-place, Blackburn, after escaping from Austrian camps, where he had been detained since the fall of Crete in 1941, told "The Lancashire Daily Post," yesterday, that he regarded the method of his escape from Austria as a closed book, and in the interests of British soldiers already held by the Germans, nothing would induce him to speak about it. On the whole, he had been fairly well treated. Red Cross parcels from home were very welcome to the boys.

He had not seen anything in the nature of revolt in any of the districts he had visited, though in some places he found an obvious hatred of the British.

Doubtless there were Germans who felt they were facing defeat, but the general feeling (as he had sensed it) was that, by some turn in fortune, they would still achieve victory. Without wireless programmes, or newspapers, he was not aware how matters stood on the Continent until he reached the British lines. Escapes from prison camps was a fairly common experience, and those who were caught had to face 21 days' what was called "field punishment." Though British prisoners were eager to get home, they were still willing to play their part in securing victory.

A married man, Gunner Oddie was a G.P.O. driver before he joined up.

THREE YEARS' ABSENCE

Recently repatriated from Switzerland, Gunner J. Lee, of 23, Garstang-road, Wesham, near Kirkham, is enjoying a spell of leave after being in captivity since December, 1941.

Joining the Army in 1940, Gunner Lee was posted to the Middle East in March, 1941. He was captured in December, 1941, and put into a prison camp near Tripoli. From Tripoli he was taken across to Italy and, after being in several camps there, was placed in a working camp near Milan.

In September, 1943, when Italy surrendered, Gunner Lee escaped from the camp.

Gunner Lee was an employee of the Kirkham Co-operative Society before joining up.

CAPTURED IN NORTH AFRICA

Paratrooper Edwin Nixon, son of Mr. and Mrs. Nixon, of 18, Mayo-street, Cockermouth, one of the 1,100 repatriated from Switzerland, was taken prisoner in North Africa and, after nine months in a camp in Italy, escaped. He spent three months in precarious liberty before crossing the border to Switzerland.

"It is no exaggeration to say," Paratrooper Nixon declares, "that had it not been for the Red Cross parcels we could not have lived."

FUGITIVES FROM NAZIS HAD GRIM STRUGGLE TO REACH SWITZERLAND

The hardships endured by British prisoners of war, in escaping from enemy prison camps to Switzerland and have been vividly described to "Lancashire Daily Post" reporters, who have interviewed a number of men from this area.

Small Union Jacks with greeting "Welcome Home" fluttered over the rambler-covered porch of the old whitewashed cottage adjoining Brock Garage, Brock, near Garstang, the home of Gunner Thomas Holmes, 25 year old son of Mr and Mrs Thomas Holmes, who has arrived home after internment in Switzerland, looking fit and well. He was one of the Service men who recently arrived at a North West port.

Gunner Holmes, who was welcomed home by his father and mother and members of the family, has had many thrilling experiences, which he unfolded to a "Lancashire Daily Post" reporter. He fought in Libya with the Eighth Army, being taken prisoner at Tobruk in June 1942. From there he was sent Tripoli, where, he says, the living conditions were then deplorable. There was a lot a casualties through lack of water, many dying of dysentery and starvation.

Food was so scarce that prisoners even sacrificed their private treasures, such as watches and rings to get it. Parcels from the Red Cross had not then got through.

Gunner Holmes was in concentration camps in Italy for 18 months before making his escape the day after the Italian capitulation. "We crossed several rivers and made good our escape into Switzerland. We tramped over hundred of miles which took two week, and had many narrow escapes from Fascists and German troops.

For two months in a prison camp and another two months after my escape I was barefoot, but on getting into Switzerland I managed to get a pair of boots, but they were much too small for me.

"My feet were swollen and tender with being without boots so long, and it was not long before I was minus four toe nails and two sore heels and a septic ankle. I crawled over the Alps on my hands and knees, as my feet were so sore. After being interrogated on the border my pal and I were interned, and treated very well indeed. I worked in the gardens at a hotel for a time, and also did a spot of wood chopping."

RED CROSS PRAISED

Gunner Holmes who joined the Army in March, 1940, was previously employed by his brother, Mr W. H. Holmes, as a driver in cattle removing business. He cannot speak to highly of the work of the Red Cross, and thanks many local people for their kindness to himself and his parents during the time he was a prisoner and interned. He was reported missing after his capture at Tobruk, and it was six months before his parents heard of his safety through a radio message from the Vatican City.

A brother signaller James Holmes is in Holland, and his youngest brother, Private Stanley Holmes is also home on leave.

"A Closed Book"

Gunner Thos. Oddie. R.A. who has just arrived at his home in Coldstream-place, Blackburn, after escaping from Austrian Camps, where he had once been detained since the fall of Crete in 1941, told the "Lancashire Daily Post" yesterday that he regarded the method of his escape from Austria as a closed book and in the interests of British soldiers already held by the Germans, nothing would induce him to speak about it. On the whole he had been fairly well treated. Red Cross parcels from home were very welcome to the boys.

He had not seen anything in the nature of revolt in any of the districts he had visited, though in some places he found an obvious hatred of the English.

Doubtless there were Germans who felt they were facing defeat, but the general feeling (as he had sensed it) was that by some turn in fortune, they would still achieve victory. Without wireless programmes, or newspapers, he was not aware how matters stood on the Continent until he reached the British lines. Escapes from prison camps was a fairly common experience, and those who were caught had to face 21 days' what was called 'field punishment' Though British prisoners were eager to get home, they were still willing to play their part in securing victory. A married man, Gunner Oddie was a G.P.O. driver before he joined up.

* * * THREE YEARS' ABSENCE * * *

Recently repatriated from Switzerland, Gunner J. Lee of 33 Garstang Road, Wesham, near Kirkham, is enjoying a spell of leave after being in captivity since December 1941.

Joining the Army in 1940, Gunner Lee was posted to the Middle East in March 1941. He was captured in December 1941 and put into a prison camp near Tripoli. From Tripoli he was taken across to Italy and after being in several camps there, was placed in a working camp near Milan.

In September 1943 when Italy surrendered Gunner Lee escaped from camp. Gunner Lee was an employee of the Kirkham Co-operative Society before joining up.

CAPTURED IN NORTH AFRICA

Paratrooper Edwin Nixon, son of Mr and Mrs Nixon of 18 Mayo Street, Cockermouth, one of the 1,100 repatriated from Switzerland was taken prisoner in North Africa and after nine months in a camp in Italy, escaped. He spent three months in precarious liberty before crossing the boarder to Switzerland.

"It is no exaggeration to say" Paratrooper Nixon declares "that had it not been for the Red Cross parcels we could not have lived"

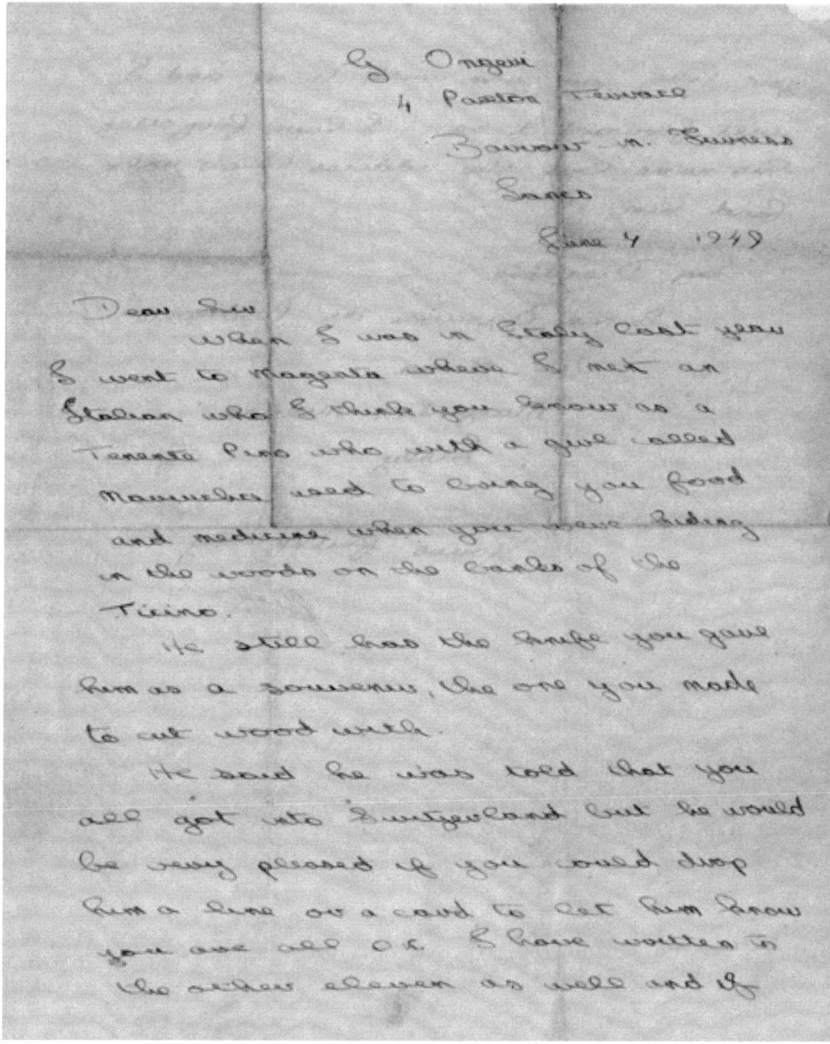

G Ongari
4 Paston Terrace
Barrow-in-Furness
Lancs
June 4 1949

Dear Sir
When I was in Italy last year I went to Maggiora where I met an Italian who I think you know as a Tenente Pino who with a girl called Mariuccia used to bring you food and medicine when you were hiding in the woods on the banks of the Ticino.
He still has the knife you gave him as a souvenir, the one you made to cut wood with.
He said he was told that you all got into Switzerland but he would be very pleased if you could drop him a line or a card to let him know you are all O.K. I have written to the other eleven as well and if

Letter about Italian guide

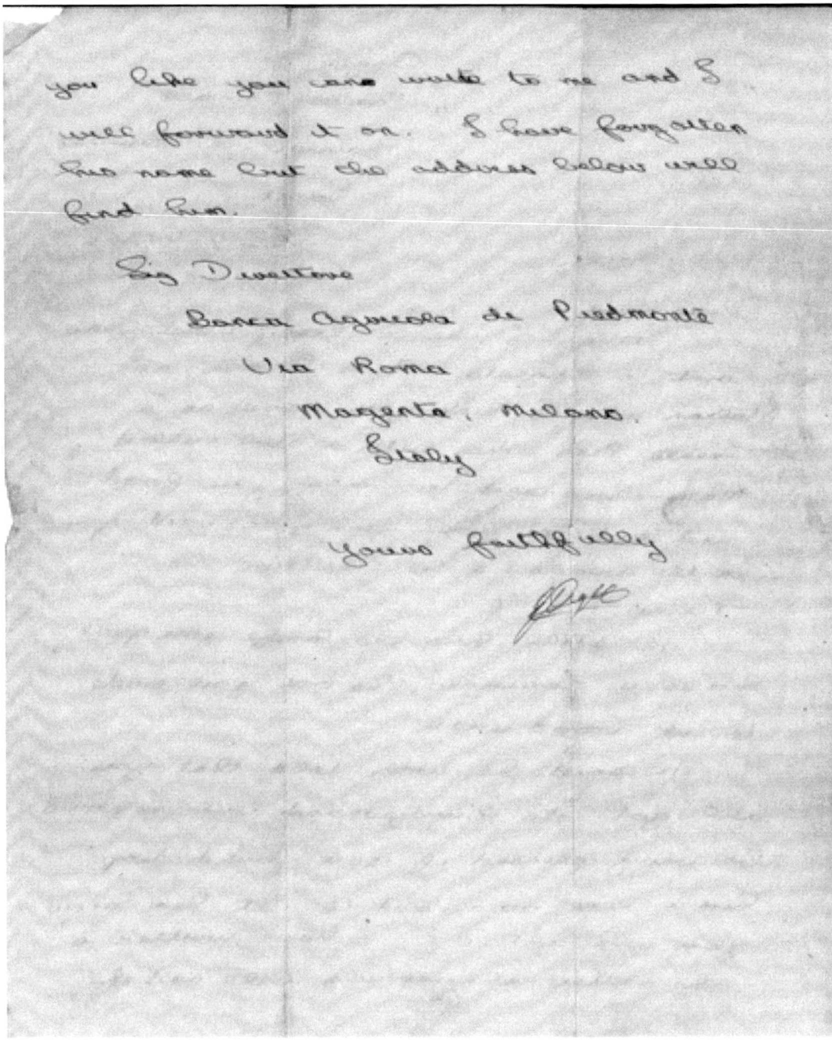

you like you can write to me and I
will forward it on. I have forgotten
his name but the address below will
find him.

Sig Direttore
Banca Agricola di Piedmonte
Via Roma
Magenta, Milano
Italy

Yours faithfully

Letter about Italian guide

EPILOGUE

"Wake up Jack, it's nearly bedtime. I thought you were sorting something out for James, not sleeping."

"I have got some bits for him, he should be suited with these. Good gracious I didn't know it was that time, I must have just dropped off."

POST SCRIPT

Back in civvy street, Jack utilised his motoring skills by driving for the Ambulance Service, the Fire Service (rising to Chief Fire Officer at Wesham) and a local undertaker, and taxi firm.

Both of Jack's brothers survived the war; Bill as a corporal fought in Italy at Monte Casino and in Greece. Bob also fought in Italy.

John Lee
Died 9th November 2003 aged 83
Beloved husband of Clara
A loving father and grandfather

Clara Lee
Died 15th May 2004 aged 79
Beloved wife of John
A loving mother and grandmother